I0759641

EPIC HISTORY OF THE
INCAS

PICHONCITO

EPIC HISTORY OF THE INCAS

Editor: Adriana Roca
Coordinating Editor: Karina Villalba
Research and Composition: Yesenia Silva
Art Direction: Raquel Tudela
Design and Illustration: Melissa Siles
Translation: Laura Healy
Layout: Andrea Wilson
Copy Editor: María Fe Carranza
Style Editor: Jorge Cornejo
Museo de Arte de Lima (MALI) Editorial Committee:
Cecilia Pardo
Julio Rucabado
Patricia Villanueva
Ricardo Kusunoki
Sharon Lerner
vm& estudio gráfico
Historical Advisor: Ricardo Guerrero

Edited by Ediciones Pichoncito S. A. C.
Jr. Santa Rosa 359, Barranco, Lima, Peru
www.pichoncito.pe
R. U. C. 20603234643

First Edition: May 2025
Print Run: 3,000 copies
Printed at Corporate Graphics Commercial
1750 Northway Drive
North Mankato, MN 56003
United States

May 2025
ISBN: 978-612-4450-61-7
Legal deposit at the National Library of Peru n.º 2024-12355

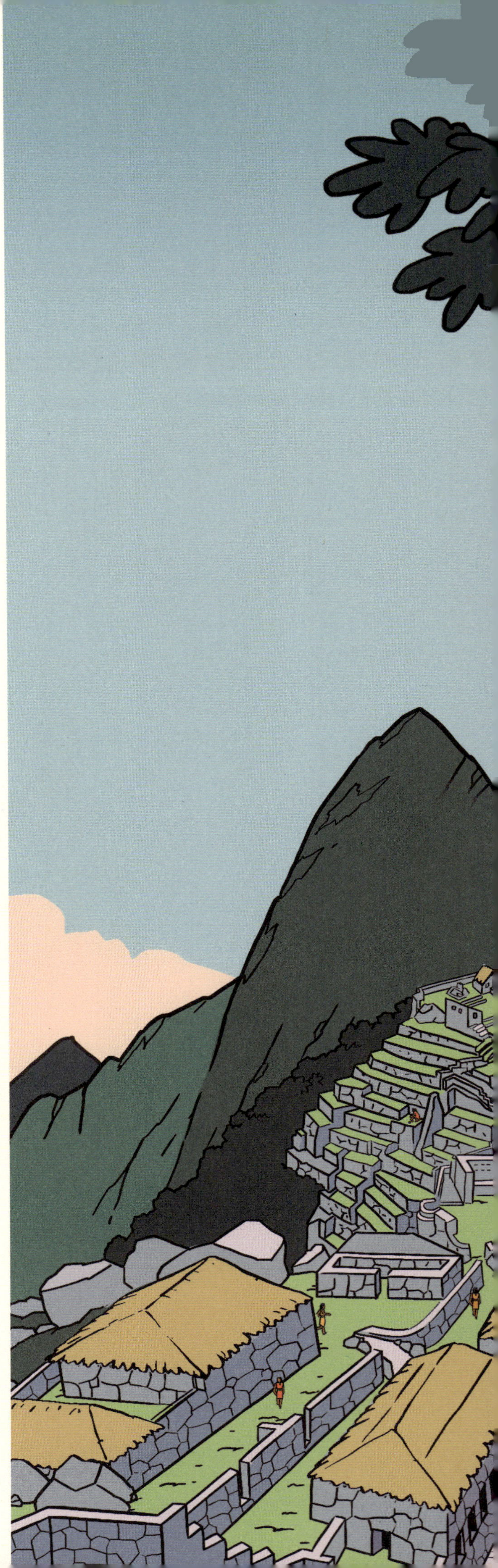

EPIC HISTORY OF THE INCAS

Human history has been shaped by the world's empires. The Assyrians, Babylonians, Persians, Greeks, Romans, Mongols, Chinese, Austro-Hungarians, Mayans, Aztecs, and many others left behind enduring legacies. We admire and study their myths, temples, fortresses, clothing, songs, poems, and artwork in the hopes of better understanding who we are and where our civilization is headed.

The most formidable empire in the history of South America emerged from the Valley of Cuzco, in the heart of Peru. Stretching from Quito (Ecuador), in the north, all the way to the Maule River (Chile), in the south, it accomplished astonishing military, technological, political, architectural, and artistic feats. It was an empire that flourished for 100 years and finally collapsed—like countless others—over a war of succession, mounting unrest between the ethnic groups under its control, and the arrival to its lands of foreigners with unknown weapons, illnesses, and animals. It was an empire that we have admired and studied for many years and whose mysteries we will continue unraveling for many years to come. It was an empire whose legacy has been recognized in World Heritage Sites. It was the Incan Empire, also known as Tahuantinsuyo.

In 2023, the Museo de Arte de Lima (MALI) assembled an unprecedented exhibition of Incan artefacts in its homeland, Peru. Thoroughly backed by the most recent research, the exhibition invited the public to rediscover the past, revisit old conceptions, and feel closer to the Incas in all their vibrant energy and most authentic humanity.

The team at Ediciones Pichoncito and Pichoncito Fly Books is honored to have collaborated with the MALI and with esteemed researchers, archaeologists, and historians in the production of *Epic History of the Incas*, a book that will accompany the exhibition on its tour, introducing children from all over the world to the achievements, challenges, successes, and defeats of this dazzling empire.

Every history begins with a story, and this story begins in one of the highest lakes in the world, when a man and a woman, children of the Sun, took up a golden staff. It is the history of the Incas—an epic history.

Pichoncito Fly Books

Lima, May 2025

Index

INTRODUCTION

How to Use This Book 5
What Happened in the World Between 500 and 1600 CE? 6
Who Were the Incas? 8

MYTHOLOGY

The Myth of Manco Capac and Mama Ocllo 10
The Myth of the Ayar Siblings 12

CULTURAL HERITAGE

The First Incas 14
Before Tahuantinsuyo 16

FORMATION AND ADMINISTRATION

The Formation of Tahuantinsuyo 18
The Great Rulers 20
Quipus and Imperial Administration 22

AGRICULTURE

Agricultural Technology 24
The Incan Laboratory at Moray 26

ART AND BELIEFS

The Sacred World 28
Art and Beliefs 30
The Art of Weaving 32
All That Glitters Is (Not) Gold... 34

EXPANSION

The Incan Army 36
Qhapaq Ñan: The Great Inca Road 38

ARCHITECTURE

Great Structures 40
The Sayhuite Stone 42
Incan Palaces and Royal Estates 44
Machu Picchu! 46

INVASION

How Did the Spanish Get to Peru? 48
The Fall of Tahuantinsuyo 50
Incan Resistance 52

THE COLONY

The Incas According to the Chronicles 54
Life in the Viceroyalty of Peru 56

THE INCAS TODAY

Remembering the Incas Today 58

Glossary 60
Bibliography 62

How to Use This Book

How did the Incan Empire begin? Who created it and why? How did it become the largest empire in South America? What were its most important monuments? In *Epic History of the Incas*, we'll bring you closer to the marvelous and expansive world of the Incas so that you can answer all these questions. This book can be read sequentially, like a long story with a beginning and an end. But you can also open up to any page to learn about a single aspect of the Incan world—for example, their architecture or their clothing. You can come back to this book again and again and discover something new each time. Below, we'll explain the different kinds of information and symbols you'll find throughout the book.

MAIN TEXT
Here you'll find basic information about the subject presented on the two-page spread.

INTERESTING DATES AND FACTS
You'll find a detailed description of a date of particular significance to the subject discussed on the two-page spread.

ARCHAEOLOGIST'S NOTES
Significant archaeological information is highlighted so you can study it like an archaeologist. These key elements reveal details about the past and help you better understand it.

ZOOM
A closer look at an image or symbol that has special significance to the subject discussed on the two-page spread.

SNAPSHOTS
Here you'll find images of the Incan world or portraits of those who were involved in it!

QUESTIONS!
This section poses questions to help you reflect on, think about, or discuss the topic at hand.

What Happened in the World Between 500 and 1600?

To help us understand the Incas and how important they were, we can look at what was going on in the rest of the world while they were building their empire. This timeline—which covers about 1,000 years—highlights important milestones of the Incan Empire, placing them alongside the most significant events in human history. (Remember that people have only been on Earth for about 300,000 years!).

476 Roman Emperor Romulus Augustulus is deposed. Odoacer, commander of the Roman Army, proclaims himself king of Italy. This marks the end of the Roman Empire and the beginning of the Middle Ages.

632 (June 8) Muhammad, the founder of Islam, dies. With his work and that of his followers, Islam spreads throughout the Middle East and North Africa.

800 (Christmas) Charlemagne is crowned *imperator augustus* by Pope Leo III. This solidifies the new political order in Europe in the period after the fall of the Roman Empire and legitimizes the Germanic tribes living in former Roman territories.

250–900 The Classic Period of Mayan civilization, during which they build administrative centers, construct great pyramids and monuments, develop writing systems, and perfect a remarkably precise calendar.

1095–1291 The Crusades, a series of nine military campaigns, are carried out by European Christians against Muslim people in order to uphold Christianity in the Holy Land (the Near East).

c. 11th Century Viking explorer Leif Eriksson arrives on the coast of Newfoundland (Canada). Viking settlements on the American continent are short-lived.

1184 The Germanic empire founded by the Saxons in the year 962 becomes known as the Holy Roman Empire.

1206 Genghis Khan unifies the Mongol tribes and begins the process of imperial expansion. Around 1276, the Mongol Empire reaches its maximum extent, encompassing the regions of China, Mesopotamia, Persia, eastern Europe, northern India, southern Russia, and beyond.

1209 Francis of Assisi founds the Order of Friars Minor (Franciscans) in Italy. In 1215, Dominic de Guzmán founds the Order of Preachers (Dominicans) in Toulouse.

1271 Beginning of Marco Polo's travels on the Silk Road (crossing Asia all the way to China).

1300–1400 The Plague or Black Death spreads across Europe, killing one-third of the continent's population.

1304–1321 Dante Alighieri writes his *Comedy* (posthumously titled the *Divine Comedy*), one of the great works of world literature.

1368 The Great Wall of China, begun in the fifth century, enters its most significant phase of construction during the Ming dynasty.

1405 and 1433 Chinese Admiral Zheng He, commissioned by the Yongle emperor (Ming dynasty), travels across the Indian Ocean and arrives at the African coast. This marks the beginning of a series of maritime voyages during which the era's most powerful state will collect tribute and establish trade routes.

1415 The Kingdom of Portugal captures Ceuta (in Northern Africa), the first step in its expansion into Madeira, the Azores, and various points along the African coast. This begins a period of extensive European maritime exploration and establishes the trade of gold and slaves with the African kingdoms.

1428 The Mexicas, as the Aztecs called themselves, establish the Triple Alliance with the Acolhuas in Texcoco and the Tepanecs in Tlacopan. In less than a century, they establish dominance over several hundred city-states in the Valley of Mexico and its surroundings.

c. 1450 Johannes Gutenberg invents the modern movable-type printing press.

1453 The invasion of Constantinople by the Ottoman Turkish army marks the end of the Byzantine Empire (or Eastern Roman Empire) and strengthens Islam in this part of the European continent.

1492 The Emirate of Granada (the last Muslim state in the Iberian peninsula) is conquered by the armies of Spain's Christian rulers.

1492 Christopher Columbus arrives in San Salvador and discovers America for the Europeans. He first has to convince the Catholic Monarchs (Isabella of Castile and Ferdinand of Aragon) that his project is viable; they finance his westward maritime expedition in hopes of finding a new route to the Asian continent. [See pages 48–49.]

1493 Pope Alexander VI, in the Alexandrine Bulls, grants the Spanish Crown the right to conquer the territories of the New World in exchange for their agreement to convert the conquered populations.

500–1100 The Tiwanaku use sophisticated agricultural techniques in the Altiplano (high plateau). [See pages 14–15.]

600–900 The Wari State becomes the first great empire of the Andes.

c. 800 The Wari of Ayacucho move into the region of Paruro (Cuzco) and build the administrative center at Piquillacta.

800–1000 The kingdoms of Chimu and Lambayeque begin to develop along the northern coast.

c. 1000 Piquillacta is abandoned.

c. 1100 Communities like the Antas, Ayarmacas, Pinahua, and Cuzcos (Incas) develop independently in the Valley of Cuzco and its surroundings. The Incas, located on the valley floor, begin forming strategic alliances with other groups, which helps them expand and grow stronger. Their military capabilities surpass those of their neighbors. [See pages 16–17.]

1200 Incan rule begins in Cuzco, and their territory expands through alliances (forced and voluntary) with the *curacas* of other ethnic groups. This gives them access to a workforce and, with it, the possibility of cultivating more fertile land. [See pages 16–17.]

1250–1440 The community of the Chancas develops in the central sierra.

1300–1400 The Incan State is reorganized during the governments of Capac Yupanqui, Inca Roca and Yahuar Huacac.

c. 1430–1450 The Incan civilization begins its imperial expansion under Pachacuti, who organizes and consolidates the state. [See page 20.]

1440–1470 In Tahuantinsuyo, work begins on important buildings like Sacsayhuamán, Coricancha, and Machu Picchu. [See pages 40–41, 44–45, 46–47.]

1524 The Inca Huayna Capac dies, apparently from illnesses brought by the Spanish. [See pages 20–21, 50–51.]

1524–1532 Huascar and Atahualpa fight for control of the Incan Empire. [See pages 20–21, 50–51.]

At what point in history did the Incan Empire arise? Where does it fit into the story of human development?

15th–16th Centuries The Renaissance, a cultural movement (artistic, philosophical, and scientific) characterized by the resurgence of classical Greek and Roman cultures, the spread of humanist ideas, and a renewed interest in knowledge.

1513 An expedition led by Vasco Núñez de Balboa crosses the isthmus of Panama and lands on the shores of the Pacific Ocean. This opens up new routes to explore the continent's south, eventually leading to their arrival in what will come to be known as Peru. Francisco Pizarro takes part in this expedition. [See pages 48–49.]

1517 Martin Luther nails his *Ninety-five Theses* to the door of the Castle Church in Wittenberg. The disputation lays out his objections to papal authority and the practices of the Catholic Church. Luther's criticisms give rise to the protestant Reformation, which divides the Church in Europe.

1519 Hernando Cortés arrives in Aztec territory. The Spanish, who are received with hospitality in Tenochtitlán, reciprocate by capturing the emperor Montezuma. The Mexicas' response compels the Spanish to abandon the city with heavy losses, but they manage to reorganize, receiving reinforcements and allying themselves with the Tlaxcaltecas (enemies of the Aztecs). After months of siege, on August 13, 1521, the conquistadores and their allies victoriously enter Tenochtitlán.

1519 Leonardo da Vinci finishes the *Mona Lisa*.

1522 The Magellan-Elcano expedition circumnavigates Earth for the first time in history.

1524 In Panama, Francisco Pizarro, Diego de Almagro, and Hernando de Luque (on behalf of the wealthy Gaspar de Espinoza) join forces. This same year, Pizarro and Almagro depart on an initial voyage that will make way for the future conquest of the Incan Empire. [See pages 48–49.]

1534 Breaking ties with the Catholic Church—which had blocked him from divorcing his first wife—King Henry VIII of England marries his consort, Anne Boleyn. He creates the Anglican Church.

1534 The French navigator and explorer Jacques Cartier arrives in the far northern territories of America (the Gulf of Saint Lawrence, Canada). This is the beginning of French presence in North America.

1534 The Society of Jesus (the Jesuit Order) is founded. It is approved by Pope Paul III in 1540.

1542 King Charles V issues the *New Laws of the Indies for the Good Treatment and Preservation of the Indians.*

1542 The explorer Francisco de Orellana launches an expedition which results in the discovery of the Amazon River.

1543 Nicolaus Copernicus publishes his work *De revolutionibus orbium coelestium*, in which he proposes that Earth is not the center of the universe but rather revolves around the sun.

1556 The Mughal emperor Akbar the Great assumes the throne in India and begins expanding his empire.

1558 Elizabeth I, one of the most important queens in the history of England, arrives on the throne.

1559 The conflicts between France and Spain come to an end. The Spanish King Philip II marries the French princess Elizabeth of Valois.

1563 The conclusion of the Council of Trent, whose decrees will play a large role in defining the Catholic response (Counter-Reformation) to the advance of Protestantism.

1568 The beginning of the Eighty Years' War, in which the provinces of the Netherlands seek independence from Spain.

1571 Muslims and Christians face off in the Battle of Lepanto; Miguel de Cervantes participates.

1588 The Invincible Armada (Spanish) is defeated by English forces. The expedition had been organized by King Phillip II as part of his plan to invade England.

1590 The sovereign Toyotomi Hideyoshi unifies the Japanese nation, which had made cultural contact with the West during this century due to the arrival of Portuguese sailors.

1603 English writer William Shakespeare publishes *Hamlet*, one of the world's great works of drama.

1605 One of the most famous works of Spanish literature is published: *Don Quixote de la Mancha* by Miguel de Cervantes.

1607 Establishment of the Virginia colony, the first permanent English settlement in North America.

c. 1609 Galileo Galilei invents the first simple telescope.

1609 *Royal Commentaries of the Incas* by Garcilaso de la Vega is published in Spain. [See page 10.]

1531–1532 An expedition led by Francisco Pizarro disembarks on the Peruvian coast and captures the Inca Atahualpa in Cajamarca. [See pages 48–49.]

1533 Atahualpa is executed by the Spanish conquistadores. [See pages 50–51.]

1536 Manco Inca, Atahualpa's nephew, rebels against the invaders and lays siege to Cuzco. After his defeat, he takes refuge at Vilcabamba. [See pages 52–53.]

1542 The Viceroyalty of Peru is established with its capital in Lima. It governs over the greater part of Spanish lands in South America.

1551 The University of San Marcos, the first in the Americas, is founded in Lima.

1569 Viceroy Francisco de Toledo arrives in Peru and puts into place the new colonial system. [See page 58.]

1570 The Tribunal of the Holy Office of the Inquisition opens in the city of Lima.

1572 After forty years of Indigenous resistance in Vilcabamba, the Inca Túpac Amaru I is captured and executed. [See page 52.]

1579 The English privateer Sir Francis Drake lays siege to the coast of the Viceroyalty of Peru and attacks ships anchored in the Port of Callao.

1615 Felipe Guamán Poma de Ayala finishes writing and illustrating his *New Chronicle and Good Government*, which is addressed to the king of Spain. [See page 54.]

Who Were the Incas?

The Incas were the founders of one of the most important empires of the ancient world. It was called Tahuantinsuyo, which means "four regions united," and it was home to at least 6 million people who belonged to different communities and ethnic groups. This enormous territory was connected by a network of roads more than twenty thousand miles long. Its rulers considered themselves children of the sun god, who—according to legend—had them build Cuzco to be the capital of the realm.

But how much do we really know about the Incas? We don't even have a detailed record of what they looked like because there were no photographs in Tahuantinsuyo, the empire's artists didn't paint portraits or make sculptures of the Incas, and they didn't leave behind any writings about themselves. However, during the early years of independence in Peru, the artist Marcos Chillitupa painted a folding screen with portraits of the ancient leaders, even though he'd never met them.

The earliest chronicles were written during the colonial period and were based on Andean oral tradition. Until then, the Incas had preserved their history through stories told to children by their parents and grandparents. These stories were written down by chroniclers: soldiers, priests, or officials of the Spanish Crown who barely knew the Andean language and culture. As they passed from speech to writing, different versions of the same stories were invented, and on more than one occasion, these stories were taken to be historical facts.

The chronicles made the Incan rulers out to be local versions of the kings and emperors of Europe. And thus an image of them began to emerge, one which has continued to develop over time, captivating researchers and explorers of all ages from around the world.

And how about you? How do you imagine them?

* Illustration based on *Genealogía de los incas (Genealogy of the Incas)*. 1837. Marcos Chillitupa Chávez. Collection of the Museo de Arte de Lima.

DAUGHTER OF THE SUN
Of the 18 portraits on Chillitupa's folding screen, 14 are the rulers of Tahuantinsuyo, according to the information provided by various chroniclers. The only woman who appears among them is Mama Ocllo, *coya* or principal wife of Manco Capac, the first Incan ruler. According to the legend that carries their names, they founded the Incan culture together. (See pages 10–11.)

* Illustration based on *Los funerales de Atahualpa (Atahualpa's Funeral)*, 1867. Luis Montero. Ignacio Merino Municipal Art Gallery, Metropolitan Municipality of Lima, housed at the Museo de Arte de Lima.
* Illustration based on *La Santusa (The Sanctuary)*, 1928. José Sabogal. Collection of the Museo de Arte de Lima.

NOT SO BARBARIC
In Garcilaso's telling, the people who came before Tahuantinsuyo seem barbaric and savage compared to the civilization of the Incas. In reality, the Incas had to compete for control of the region with various groups who all had similar levels of development, like the Collas from the Lake Titicaca basin and the Chancas who occupied what is now the Andahuaylas region.

The Myth of Manco Capac and Mama Ocllo

Every civilization has a story to explain its origin. In the case of the Incas, there are two major myths or legends, one of which is the story of Manco Capac and Mama Ocllo. When the chronicler Garcilaso de la Vega—son of an Incan princess and a Spanish conquistador—was a boy, he would listen to his maternal uncles recounting the history of his ancestors' great empire: Tahuantinsuyo. One day, he approached the oldest one and asked, "Uncle, who was the first Inca? Where did he come from?" And he was told the following story:

Out of Lake Titicaca emerged Manco Capac and Mama Ocllo, children of the sun god. He had sent them to the land with a mission: to organize his people and make them prosper. He gave them a golden staff and told them to walk north and, every so often, to drive the staff into the ground. Wherever the staff sank into the earth was where they should stay and found their empire. When they arrived at the hill of Huanacaure, in Cuzco, the staff pierced the ground so swiftly and easily that it was never seen again. Manco Capac and Mama Ocllo decided to settle there and build a temple in honor of the Sun. On seeing this, the people of the Valley of Cuzco wished to join them and make them their leaders. In exchange, the couple taught them how to plant and cultivate the land, how to spin and weave to make clothing and shoes, how to build houses and irrigation canals, and everything else they needed to live better lives.

Written by Garcilaso and published in 1609, this became one of the most popular myths, but there are other versions of the Incas' origin story. The oldest are mythical stories like this one, recorded by Spanish chroniclers during the colonial period. More recent versions are possible explanations by historians and archeologists, who are still trying to figure out who the first Incas were and how they got to Cuzco.

WHY DO ANCIENT PEOPLE HAVE MYTHS?

Throughout history, most human groups have told tales (myths and legends) to explain the origins of the world and what goes on in it, especially those situations that are beyond common sense and understanding. Using characters like gods, heroes, and creatures with supernatural powers, societies imagine how the world was created and the origins of their people and of humanity in general. Even though myths and legends don't tell historic facts, they do reflect the way of thinking of those who create them.

CREATION MYTHS

To explain their origins and extend their influence in the Andes, the Incas came up with tales of fantastic events and ancestral heroes, like Manco Capac and Mama Ocllo. These stories reinforced the idea that their rulers were children of the Sun and therefore superior to other chiefs in the region.

The Myth of the Ayar Siblings

The other great myth about the birth of the Incan Empire is the story of the Ayar siblings. There are many versions of this story about four brothers and their wives who take a journey across the Andes. The one recounted here was written by Juan de Betanzos shortly after the conquest of Tahuantinsuyo. Betanzos was a Spanish soldier who lived for a long time in Cuzco, learned Quechua so well he became an interpreter, and married an Incan noblewoman named Angelina Yupanqui. She and her relatives were surely the ones who told him this fantastic story:

The legend goes that on a hillside, seven leagues from Cuzco, a cave opened up that was so narrow you could only get in and out of it on hands and knees. It was called Pacaritambo, which means "house of production." That day, four couples were born there, by the hand of Viracocha, creator of the universe. The first to appear were Ayar Cachi and Mama Huaco. After them, Ayar Uchu and Mama Cora, followed by Ayar Auca and Mama Ragua. The last to emerge were Ayar Manco and Mama Ocllo. The eight of them were dressed in the finest wool, with gold trimmings and embroidery.

The men were armed with gold lances and slingshots. The women carried pots, small jugs, plates and cups—all made of gold. They arrived on foot at the hill of Huanacaure. From its peak, Ayar Cachi launched stones with his slingshot, using so much force that he broke the hills apart. Seeing this, the other brothers were frightened and decided to lock him up in Pacaritambo, so they tricked him into returning there. No sooner had Ayar Cachi entered the cave than they covered the entrance with a huge stone.

The seven who remained decided to continue on to Cuzco, but first Ayar Uchu took the shape of a bird and flew into the sky to speak with their father, the Sun. He returned with instructions to change Ayar Manco's name to Manco Capac. Then he turned into a stone idol and stayed on Huanacaure. Ayar Auca and Manco Capac continued on, but along the way Ayar Auca also turned to stone. The only ones left were Manco Capac and the four women, who finally arrived in Cuzco, where they found a group of people living in rustic houses. The leader of the group, seeing them so well dressed and ornamented, knew that they were children of the Sun and invited them to stay wherever they liked. And that is how the first Incas established themselves in the valley, where they planted corn and made their home.

COLCAMPATA
ACAMA
CUSCO
HUANACAURE
YAURISQUI
TAMBO
TOCO
PALLATA
PACARITAMBO
1 LEAGUE = 1 HOUR'S WALK
DID YOU KNOW THAT A LEAGUE IS AN ANCIENT WAY OF MEASURING THE DISTANCE TRAVELED ON FOOT OR ON HORSEBACK? ONE LEAGUE EQUALS ONE HOUR OF WALKING. THAT'S WHY ITS LENGTH DIFFERS BY COUNTRY OR REGION AND CAN VARY FROM 2 TO 4 MILES.
THE POWERFUL MAMA HUACO
BETANZOS TELLS US THAT MAMA HUACO, THE WIFE OF AYAR CACHI, WAS SO FEROCIOUS THAT SHE FRIGHTENED THE LOCALS OF A SMALL TOWN, CAUSING THEM TO FLEE IN TERROR. IN OTHER VERSIONS OF THE STORY, SHE APPEARS AS THE CAPTAIN OF HER OWN ARMY, A FEARED WARRIOR, AND A POWERFUL SORCERESS.
LA PRIMERA HISTORIA DE LAS REINAS COIA
MAMA VACO COIA
FANTASTIC PLACES
SOME OF THE PLACES MENTIONED IN THE INCAN ORIGIN STORIES ARE PLACES WE CAN ACTUALLY VISIT IN THE REGION AROUND CUZCO, LIKE MAUCALLACTA. NEVERTHELESS, RESEARCHERS HAVEN'T BEEN ABLE TO PROVE THAT THESE STORIES ARE HISTORICAL FACTS OR THAT THE CHARACTERS WHO APPEAR IN THEM REALLY EXISTED.
MAUCALLACTA
AYAR UCHU

The First Incas

Now we enter the realm of history, of what really happened and how. Several centuries after the disappearance of two great states—Wari in Ayacucho and Tiwanaku near lake Titicaca—the Incas became the primary civilization of the central Andean region. The Tiwanaku developed various technologies to improve their crops, which produced abundant food despite the dry, cold climate of the Altiplano (high plateau), with its droughts and deep frosts. The Wari were excellent at administration, for which they developed the famous system of cords and knots that was also used by the Incas: *quipus*. The Wari occupied a broad territory and built urban administrative centers. One of the most well-known is Piquillacta, which you can visit in the Valley of Cuzco.

These empires dominated much of the Andes for more than 400 years, until both came to an end around the year 1000. At that time, various groups of farmers and shepherds were living in the Cuzco region. Some lived on the hilltops, where they could defend themselves against whoever might attack them. Others, like the Incas, started populating the valley floor, a strategic area for cultivating the land and producing more and better harvests. They managed to store enough food to feed not only their own community but also other groups that joined them. Using this strategy, the great Incan settlement started to grow, bit by bit, until it became the largest in the region.

Researchers can imagine what life was like for the Incas by studying the objects they produced and used. Large quantities of ceramics in a style called Killke have been found beneath important imperial buildings like Sacsayhuamán and Coricancha, as well as in the center of the city of Cuzco. By studying these artefacts, it has been determined that the Incan State formed during this period, much earlier than the Spaniards who wrote the first chronicles had thought.

AYACUCHO

HUARI CITY
This administrative center was surrounded by walls, inside of which were neighborhoods containing houses, palaces, courtyards, and D-shaped temples.

CUZCO

PIQUILLACTA
Piquillacta's gridded design was reproduced in various Wari settlements along the sierra. In Quechua, *piki* means "flea" and *llacta* means "city," so Piquillacta is the "city of fleas"!

LIMA

PACHACAMAC
The Wari acquired this prestigious religious center sometime around the year 600, and they used it as a cemetery for important groups. It was occupied by the Incas toward the end of the 15th century.

A GREAT STATE BEFORE THE INCAS
WARI, A GREAT STATE REACHING ALL THE WAY TO CAJAMARCA IN THE NORTH AND MOQUEGUA IN THE SOUTH, EMERGED IN THE SIERRA OF AYACUCHO
MORE THAN 1500 YEARS AGO. ITS POPULATION WAS CONCENTRATED IN WELL-PLANNED SETTLEMENTS WITH THEIR OWN UNIQUE STYLE.
ANCESTRAL ROADS
It's likely that some of the roads constructed by the Wari served as the base of the Inca Road or Qhapaq Ñan.

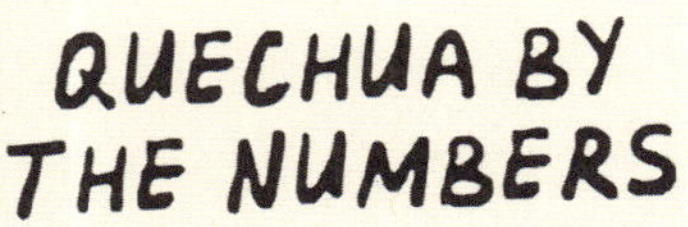

TODAY, SEVEN MILLION PEOPLE SPEAK QUECHUA ACROSS FIVE SOUTH AMERICAN COUNTRIES: COLOMBIA, ECUADOR, PERU, BOLIVIA, AND ARGENTINA. IN PERU, THERE ARE ALMOST FOUR MILLION QUECHUA SPEAKERS.

QUILLISCACHES

By living at fortified sites like Huata, which was built on a mountaintop and surrounded by a great wall, the Quilliscaches were able to maintain their independence for many years.

AYARMACAS

One of the largest and most powerful groups, the Ayarmacas—like their neighbors, the Antas—chose to ally themselves with the Incas rather than make war with them. Mama Chicya, wife of the Inca Yahuar Huacac, was the daughter of an Ayarmaca.

Before Tahuantinsuyo

The formation of Tahuantinsuyo was a long process that began several centuries before 1400, when the communities living in the valley and its surroundings either joined the first Incas voluntarily or surrendered to them by force. As the population had grown, different groups had started competing amongst themselves for the territory's resources. The first Incas, who had settled in the valley, were able to gather many communities under their control, but their strongest neighbors either resisted or moved to faraway places where they could more easily defend themselves.

The first groups to join the Incas began identifying with them and assimilating into their culture. Among them were the Antas, the Ayarmacas, and the Huayllacan, who settled their conflicts with the young Incan State by uniting their families in arranged marriages. By around the year 1300, an important cultural center had formed, integrating more than twelve Andean communities. That's when construction began on a large capital city, in Cuzco, where the Incas' own architectural style emerged.

Nevertheless, in the Lucre River basin, the Pinahua and the Mohina continued to rival the Incas for a long time. The end result of these conflicts, marriages, and alliances was the creation of a solid regional state that integrated diverse ethnic groups into a single force capable of becoming the largest empire in the Americas.

LANGUAGE, LANGUAGE, EVERYWHERE

DID YOU KNOW THE QUECHUA LANGUAGE WAS SPOKEN IN THE ANDES LONG BEFORE THE INCAS? IT MADE IT POSSIBLE FOR DIFFERENT ETHNIC GROUPS IN THE AREA TO COMMUNICATE WITH EACH OTHER: EVEN THOUGH EACH GROUP SPOKE ITS OWN LANGUAGE, QUECHUA—WHICH ARRIVED IN CUZCO SEVERAL CENTURIES EARLIER WITH THE WARI OF AYACUCHO—WAS A LANGUAGE THEY ALL HAD IN COMMON.

PINAHUA AND MOHINA
These two distinct groups were closely related. They put up quite a fight against the Incas and were some of the last to be absorbed into the empire. The Pinahua occupied the site at Choquepuquio.
CUYOS
According to some chronicles, the Incas invaded the Cuyos after their leader refused to send exotic birds from the lowland jungle to Cuzco.
HUAYLLACAN
This group fell under the Incas' control long before the expansion of Tahuantinsuyo. They first established alliances through marriage but were later dominated militarily.
MASCAS AND TAMBOS
Because they were small communities, these groups living in the southern part of the Valley of Cuzco were among the first to unite with the Incas.

The Formation of Tahuantinsuyo

Did the Incas have an empire? Were their leaders Andean kings? "Empire," "kings," "court," and "nobility" are words the Spanish brought to the Andes in 1532. The European chroniclers were the ones who used these and other words when writing the first historical accounts of the Incas.

In the early years of Tahuantinsuyo, the Incas' power and influence were becoming greater and greater. In the beginning, they avoided conflicts with other ethnic groups in the Cuzco region and put their energy into managing and improving their own economy. But as they became stronger, neighboring communities sought to ally themselves with the Incas as a defense against their rivals. Joining the Incas meant adopting the sun cult, recognizing the Incan ruler's authority over that of the local elders or *curacas*, paying taxes, and using the Quechua language.

Groups that didn't submit voluntarily were invited to become part of the young state in exchange for luxury gifts like fine *uncu* (tunics), *quero* (wooden cups), and *aquillas* (silver cups). However, if they didn't accept, they would be conquered by force. In this way, the Incas formed a confederation of Quechuan ethnic groups with a massive army that marched through the Andes on increasingly aggressive military campaigns. By the year 1500, Tahuantinsuyo was a vast community of different peoples living throughout the Andes, from the Pacific coast to the edge of the Amazon rainforest, in territories that are now part of Peru, Colombia, Ecuador, Bolivia, Chile, and Argentina.

ACCOUNTING AND RECORDKEEPING
The Incas used *quipus*, a system of cords and knots, to keep records of the population, harvests, and livestock, among other things. The *quipucamayoc* was the specialist in charge of this task.

CULT OF THE SUN GOD
The Incas spread their sun cult and made it the official state religion. They created a calendar of rituals and offerings and built temples both in Cuzco and in conquered territories. The most important temples to the sun god were in Cuzco (Coricancha), on the Island of the Sun in Lake Titicaca, and in Pachacamac (Lima).

ROAD NETWORK
Known as Qhapaq Ñan, the Inca Road was designed and built to connect the different regions of the empire. From north to south and east to west, it extended more than twenty thousand miles. It even had rest stops, called *tambos*, for the soldiers and messengers who traveled it.
ARRANGED MARRIAGES
Women of the elite were important leaders in their communities. Their marriages to Incan rulers augmented their power in the empire and also encouraged good relations between the Incas and less powerful groups.
LUXURY GIFTS
The Incas exchanged precious objects as a strategy for negotiating with the *curacas* or elders of different villages. The task of producing the fine cloth for these gifts fell to the *Mamaconas*. They were the teachers of the *acllaconas*, the women and girls selected to live in the *acllahuasis*, which means "house of the chosen ones" in Quechua.
MILITARY FORCE
The Incas formed a powerful army for which they recruited warriors from all the villages belonging to the new regime.
WHAT DOES THE WORD "INCA" MEAN?
CÕÇEJOREAL:DESTOSREINOS
CAPACIGA·TAVANTIN
SVIO·CAMACHICOC·APOCONA
BEFORE THE SPANISH ARRIVED, THE TERM "INCA" DIDN'T DEFINE AN ETHNIC GROUP OR AN ARISTOCRACY BUT RATHER A COLLECTION OF PEOPLE HAILING FROM DIFFERENT VILLAGES AND UNITED INTO A SINGLE MILITARY FORCE: THE CONQUERING INCAN ARMY.
PEOPLE WITH HIGHER STATUS CAME FROM A GROUP CALLED THE CUZCOS; HOWEVER, TAHUANTINSUYO WASN'T A MONARCHY LED BY A KING. ON THE CONTRARY, IT WAS A WELL-ORGANIZED WARRIOR SOCIETY THAT RECOGNIZED THE SUPREME AUTHORITY OF A SAPA INCA OR "UNIQUE INCA," WHO HELD ALL THE POWER AND RESPONSIBILITY OF THE ENTIRE COMMUNITY.

Great Rulers

Who were the great Incan rulers? The chroniclers tell us that Pachacuti organized the Incan State and expanded its dominions from Manta in Ecuador all the way to Sucre in Bolivia, making it into a great empire. Topa Inca Yupanqui (Túpac Yupanqui) was a skilled warrior and explorer—some believe he traveled all the way to Polynesia by sea! Huayna Capac was a great strategist who fought to maintain good relations with the groups he had conquered. His sons, Huascar and Atahualpa, battled for control and ignited a civil war that debilitated the Incan State. Even though Atahualpa beat his brother, his own defeat by the Spanish marked the beginning of the end of Tahuantinsuyo.

In contrast to the way things were done in Europe, Incan rulers didn't inherit their power automatically but were chosen from among several male candidates. They did need to meet certain requirements: be members of the Cuzco nobility, have the skills needed to govern, be able to forge and maintain good relations with other groups, and above all, have "the favor of the gods" for war and for managing resources.

The priests would announce the most suitable candidates, and members of the *panacas*—noble families descended from ancient rulers—would choose from among their recommendations. Marriage to the *coya* was an important part of this election, and the union was celebrated at the same time that the Incan ruler was officially named. From that moment on, he would become a god, capable of resolving any conflict.

These five Incan rulers are the most famous in the history of the empire. The chronicles credit them with the period of greatest expansion and power, which began with Pachacuti, about a hundred years before the Spanish invasion.

FOREVER AN INCA

AFTER THE RULERS' DEATHS, THEIR BODIES WERE PRESERVED, AND THEIR MUMMIES WERE TREATED AS IF THEY WERE ALIVE. THEY HAD SERVANTS TO CARE FOR THEIR NEEDS AND WERE CARRIED IN PROCESSION DURING BIG CELEBRATIONS. THEY EVEN TOOK PART IN BANQUETS AND VISITED OTHER TERRITORIES!

TOPA INCA YUPANQUI

The Conqueror

Cuzco, 1440–1493

- Led eight victorious campaigns of conquest, clearing the way for the empire's maximum expansion.
- Extended the territorial limits to Quito in the north and the Maule River in the south.
- After conquering the Chimu, returned to Cuzco with great riches and expert artisans.
- Took the first census of the Incan population.
- Built the fortress of Sacsayhuamán.

HUAYNA CAPAC

The Strategist

Tomebamba, 1464 – Quito, 1528

- Founded the city of Cochabamba.
- Faced various rebellions across the empire and succeeded in containing them.
- Died of small pox or measles, illnesses brought to South America by the Spanish.

HUASCAR

The Novice

Cuzco, 1503 – Ancash, 1533

- After a happy start to his reign, made enemies with his brother Atahualpa and declared war.
- Lost the support of the Cuzco nobility due to his lack of experience.
- Was defeated and captured after a series of clashes.
- Was drowned in the Ayarmaca River (modern Yanamayo) on Atahualpa's orders.

ATAHUALPA

The Last Inca

Cuzco, 1498 – Cajamarca, 1533

- Faced off against his brother with fewer men and resources; managed to defeat him regardless.
- Received news of the Spaniards' arrival on the empire's coast.
- Offered guides and provisions to Pizarro's men, never imagining what would happen next.
- Was recognized as Inca by the Cuzco nobility after Huáscar's death.

IF YOU RULED TAHUANTINSUYO...

YOU WOULD ALWAYS DRESS IN THE FINEST CLOTH AND WEAR THE MASCAYPACHA, A HEADDRESS WOVEN WITH GOLDEN THREAD AND MOUNTAIN CARACARA FEATHERS, WHICH WAS PLACED ATOP THE INCAN RULER'S HEAD TO SYMBOLIZE HIS POWER. WHEREVER YOU WENT, YOU WOULD BE ACCOMPANIED BY A GROUP OF MUSICIANS, DANCERS, AND SOLDIERS, AND YOU'D BE CARRIED ALOFT IN A LITTER. YOUR FEET COULD NEVER TOUCH THE GROUND BECAUSE IT WAS BELIEVED THAT IF THE ENORMOUS DIVINE FORCE OF THE INCA MADE CONTACT WITH THE EARTH, IT COULD CAUSE CATASTROPHE TO STRIKE.

* Illustration taken from the book *Scale and the Incas*, 2018. Andrew Hamilton. Princeton University Press.

FEAR OF THE UNKNOWN
Did you know that, in 1583, the Catholic Church banned the use of *quipus*? They did this because they considered them to be a pagan recordkeeping system, inferior to Western writing. This prohibition contributed to the loss of the knowledge needed to interpret them correctly.

DECIMAL ADMINISTRATION
The empire was made up of around eighty provinces, and each one was supervised by a *tucuyricuy* ("he who observes"), assisted by a *quipucamayoc* responsible for recording all information. To organize labor and production in each province, the Incas came up with a base-ten system: the largest groups under the administrators' supervision had ten thousand families, and the smallest had just ten families.

Quipus and Imperial Administration

Did you know that the Quechua word *quipu* means "knot"? As far back as the Wari—whose great state existed long before the Incas emerged—knotted strings were used to record all kinds of information. In Tahuantinsuyo, this system was adapted to the empire's needs and became an important part of its administration. The quipus could hold data about the number of goods, people, or workers, and they were also used to record stories and historical facts. The chronicler Pedro Cieza de León tells us that quipus worked so well that nothing could escape their recordkeeping...not even a pair of sandals!

Made of cotton fibers and camelid wool, quipus were composed of colored strings fastened to a main cord. Specific kinds of information were indicated by the number and shape of the knots and their exact position on a section of string as well as by the colors of the strings and the way they were braided. Their reading, handling, and fabrication was overseen by the *quipucamayocs*, who were in charge of supervising the conquered peoples. The information recorded in the quipus was turned over to the rulers of each of the four principal regions or *suyos*. These men, in turn, reported back to the Sapa Inca, head of the empire.

After the Spanish invasion, the Incas kept many of their traditions and beliefs, among them the use of quipus. Some villages used them for agricultural accounting all the way up to the end of the twentieth century. Even though researchers have learned a lot about their recording ability, we still don't know exactly how these colored, knotted strings held such diverse information with as much complexity as is described by various chroniclers. With the passage of time, quipus have adapted and transformed to meet the new challenges faced by the Andean world, and today they're still used in some communities as a symbol of authority and cultural heritage.

* Illustration based on the photograph *Autoridades de San Andrés de Tupicocha cargando quipus* (Authorities of San Andrés de Tupicocha Laden with Quipus), 2018. Martin Chumbe.

Agricultural Technology

Did you know the Incas' management of the land and of food production was one of the reasons their empire was able to grow so much and so quickly? For centuries, different Andean groups had been developing sustainable ways to grow and harvest food. The Incas collected this knowledge and used it to organize agricultural production across Tahuantinsuyo. Even though they didn't develop new technologies, they learned from their ancestors and managed to satisfy the needs of the approximately six million people who made up the largest empire in the Americas.

The Andes Mountains, with their complex geography, presented the Incas with many challenges. Still, this important mountain range provided a great variety of climates and landscapes—of the 104 kinds of ecosystems that exist on the planet, Peru has 84! Andean settlers knew that it was possible to extract different resources from each one of them, which is why the same group would settle in multiple regions at once. As they expanded their domain across the Andes, the Incas established ties with these groups, not only to increase the size of their territory but also to gain access to a greater variety of resources.

The Andean people used different traditional techniques depending on the land's characteristics. On the steep slopes of hills, they built platforms or agricultural terraces. In coastal valleys and in the mountains, they implemented complicated irrigation systems. In the punas (high plateaus), they used sunken fields or *cochas* to increase the farmland's humidity and raised fields or *waru warus* to protect the crops from floods. To work the land, they used tools like the *chaquitaclla* or foot plow. As fertilizer, they used guano as well as llama and alpaca manure. All of these strategies, techniques, and tools have been used in the Andes since before the Incas and are still in use today.

Nutrition in Tahuantinsuyo

The Incas' daily diet included highly nutritious foods like quinoa, amaranth, and maca. In addition to tubers, like oca and ullucu, they ate many varieties of potato. Their fruits included chirimoyas (custard apple), husk-tomatoes, guanabanas (soursop), and lucumas. The most common animal proteins were dried fish and charqui (dried llama meat).

READING NATURE

The Incas were great observers of nature and knew how to "read" the different signs they found there. For example, the location of bird's nests at lake Titicaca predicted the water level: if the nest was on high ground, the water usually rose; if not, it usually fell down. Also, the appearance of a strange circular rainbow (a halo) announced the beginning of the dry season.

WHAT IS GUANO?

This natural fertilizer, rich in nitrogen, phosphorous, and potassium, was made of the manure of marine birds like the cormorant, the Peruvian booby, the pelican, and the Inca tern. It was deposited on the coasts and offshore islands, then brought up into the mountains.

EARTH MOTHER

Pachamama or Earth Mother was an Incan goddess. She symbolized fertility and was seen as the source of life, responsible for providing good harvests.

EAT LIKE AN INCA

The Incas ate maize (corn) in many ways, and they were all delicious! When cooked in water, they called it *muti*. When toasted, they called it *camcha*. Using ground maize, they made delicious *humitas* (similar to tamales). And they also made a drink of fermented maize called *chicha*. Did you know the popcorn you eat while watching movies is also maize?

NO PRESERVATIVES

PRESERVING AND STORING FOOD WAS ONE OF THE INCAS' TOP PRIORITIES, AND THEY DEVELOPED VARIOUS METHODS OF GOING ABOUT IT. THEY PRESERVED FISH AND OTHER MEATS BY SALTING THEM AND DRYING THEM IN THE SUN. SOME GRAINS, LIKE MAIZE, WERE TOASTED AND TURNED INTO FLOUR. POTATOES WERE DEHYDRATED TO MAKE CHUÑO, WHICH COULD LAST FOR YEARS. AND LIQUIDS COULD BE STORED AS VINEGARS AND CHICHA.

The Incan Laboratory at Moray

The legend goes that the Inca Huayna Capac lived in a golden palace south of Moray, in the Urubamba Valley. Each year, the most powerful *apus* in Cuzco—ancestral spirits in the form of mountains—went to this palace to receive their farming tasks from the ruler himself. Although we don't know exactly what Moray and its impressive system of terraces were used for, one likely possibility is that it was a place for agricultural experimentation during the time of the Incas.

Moray is located on the pampa (prairie) of Maras, twenty miles from the city of Cuzco, and it is truly a sight to behold. From the air, its perfectly symmetrical circular terraces look like enormous eyes. They were built taking advantage of the ground's natural slope. These platforms, which descend into four holes or *muyus*—a word that means "circle" in Quechua—are rain resistant and never flood. This is partly because of the porous ground and partly due to canals the Incas built to direct the water's course.

At different levels on these platforms, the Incas did something that had long been done in the Andes: they experimented with different crops! Long before Tahuantinsuyo, Andean people figured out how plants grew in different climates and situations: how well they resisted freezes, droughts, floods, hot and cold years, plagues of insects, fungi, etc. On each platform or terrace, they took into account heat, sun exposure, shade, altitude, and soil. This made it possible for each one to have its own microclimate so that crops could be grown in different ways at different altitudes.

ASTRONOMICAL OBSERVATORY
Researchers believe that the key dates of the Incan calendar—which are closely tied to agriculture—are "marked" on the terraces of Moray. When the sun rises or sets during solstices and equinoxes, which signal a change of season, shadows from the hills are cast in a particular way on the platforms.

POOLS OF SALT

THE ARCHAEOLOGICAL COMPLEX AT MORAY IS FOUND IN THE TOWN OF MARAS, FAMOUS FOR ITS BLINDING WHITE SALT MINES, WHICH FORM A SPECTACULAR LANDSCAPE. IF YOU GO THERE, YOU'VE GOT TO TRY THE PRODUCTS THEY MAKE WITH THIS PINK SALT—ESPECIALLY THE CHOCOLATES!

MARAS

PLATFORMS

SINCE BEFORE THE RISE OF THE INCAS, PLATFORMS WERE USED TO TAKE ADVANTAGE OF THE STEEP SLOPES OF THE MOUNTAINS AND TO STOP EROSION ON THE HILLSIDES. BECAUSE OF THEM, THOUSANDS MORE ACRES COULD BE USED FOR AGRICULTURE.

APU MORAY
AMONG RURAL COMMUNITIES TODAY, THE SITE OF MORAY IS KNOWN AS A POWERFUL MOUNTAIN GOD CALLED APU MORAY. THE QUECHUA WORD APU, WHICH CAN BE TRANSLATED AS "LORD," WAS ALSO USED AS A TITLE FOR HIGH-RANKING INCAN GOVERNMENT OFFICIALS.
GOOD HARVESTS
THE INCAS PERFORMED RITUALS ASKING THEIR GODS FOR FERTILE CROPS AND LIVESTOCK. MANY OF THOSE RITUALS TOOK PLACE WHEN THE SEASONS CHANGED AND LINED UP WITH DATES ON THE INCAN CALENDAR, LIKE THE FESTIVAL OF CHACRA YAPUI QUILLA, WHICH IS ASSOCIATED WITH THE MOON AND CELEBRATED IN AUGUST, THE MONTH OF PLANTING.
TRAVAXOS
PAPAALLAIMITAPA
ANCESTRAL ENGINEERING
The terraces of Moray were irrigated by canals carved into their walls. Water coming into the muyus was channeled downward to each of the terraces.

JUAN DE SANTA CRUZ PACHACUTI DREW THIS PICTURE DEPICTING THE PRINCIPAL ANDEAN GODS. ALTHOUGH IT WAS DRAWN SOMETIME AROUND 1613, HE SWORE HE HAD SEEN IT WHEN HE WAS A BOY ON A GOLDEN PLAQUE LOCATED INSIDE OF CORICANCHA. (*QORI* OR *QURI* MEANS "GOLD," AND *CANCHA* REFERS TO A NEARBY ENCLOSURE; THE JOINING OF THESE TWO WORDS EXPLAINS THE CHRONICLERS' DESCRIPTIONS OF AN ENCLOSURE WITH WALLS COVERED IN PLATES OF GOLD.)

1. **VIRACOCHA:** CREATOR GOD OF THE INCAS; THIS CHARACTER MAY HAVE TAKEN ON TRACES OF THE CHRISTIAN GOD.
2. **INTI OR SUN:** THE FORCES OF NATURE WERE DIVINITIES EMBODIED IN THE FORM OF *HUACAS*. THE SUN WAS THE MAIN GOD OF TAHUANTINSUYO, DESCRIBED AS A GOLDEN IDOL IN THE SHAPE OF A CHILD. AS HIS CULT STRENGTHENED, HE TOOK ON SOME ATTRIBUTES THAT WERE PREVIOUSLY ASCRIBED TO VIRACOCHA, ARCHITECT OF THE WORLD.
3. **QUILLA OR MOON:** WIFE AND SISTER OF THE SUN, SHE WAS THE PROTECTOR OF WOMEN AND ALL THINGS FEMININE.
4. **ILLAPA OR LIGHTNING:** HIS POWER WAS MANIFESTED IN METEOROLOGICAL PHENOMENA LIKE THUNDER, LIGHTNING, RAIN, AND HAIL.
5. **STARS:** THE TWO MOST IMPORTANT WERE THE MORNING STAR OR CHASCA, THE SUN'S GUARDIAN, AND THE EVENING STAR OR CHOQUECHINCHAY, THE MOON'S WATCHMAN.
6. **PACHAMAMA OR EARTH MOTHER:** THE SOURCE OF LIFE AND FERTILITY, SHE WAS IN CHARGE OF PROVIDING GOOD HARVESTS.
7. **MAMA COCHA OR MOTHER LAKE:** GODDESS OF RIVERS, SEAS, LAKES, AND PONDS, SHE WAS IN CHARGE OF THE RAINS, FAVORABLE SEAS, AND GOOD FISHING.
8. **OTHER GODS OR *HUACAS*:** RAINBOWS, THE MILKY WAY, OTHER CELESTIAL BODIES, AND SOME ANIMALS WERE ALSO CONSIDERED DIVINE. IN ADDITION, THERE WERE CELEBRATED LOCAL AND REGIONAL GODS LIKE PACHACAMAC.
9. ***MALLQUI*:** IN QUECHUA, THE WORD *MALLQUI* MEANS "TREE" AND "ANCESTOR," AND IT WAS USED TO SHOW OUR CONNECTION TO THE PLANT LIFE CYCLE (BIRTH-GROWTH-REPRODUCTION-DEATH-REGENERATION); THE TERM ALSO APPEARS TO HAVE REFERRED TO ANCESTORS.

* Illustration taken from *Relación de las antigüedades deste Reyno del Perú* (*An Account of Ancient Times in this Kingdom of Peru*), c. 17th century. Juan de Santa Cruz Pachacuti Yamqui Salcamayhua.

Sacred World

In the Andes, the idea of a single God, creator of all things, did not exist. The Incas insisted on the worship of the Sun, but they also respected the divinities of each region, so the inhabitants of Tahuantinsuyo continued to worship their many deities. Some of the most important gods were related to the planets and forces of nature like the sun (Inti), the moon (Quilla), the stars (Chasca and Choquechinchay), and lightning (Illapa). According to the Incas, rituals connected human beings to these forces, who made life on Earth possible. The most important gods, like the Sun, had their own lands and servants across the empire who were in charge of their cult.

One word that is key to understanding the Andean religion is *huaca*, which means "sacred." The Inca, who was considered a child of the Sun, also became huaca the moment he was selected. Everything considered sacred in the time of the Incas was a huaca: not just places and people but also objects and even ancestors in the form of mummies or *mallquis* (Quechua for "ancestors"). Today, many archeological sites are called huaca because they were sacred places in the past.

The *mallquis* mentioned in the chronicles were mostly the mummies of dead Incan rulers. Their descendants took care of them, revered them, and even asked them for advice. The lands that had belonged to them were passed down to their *panaca* or family group, who took charge of all their ancestors' responsibilities and obligations. And so the *mallquis* continued holding banquets, exchanging gifts, and being an important part of the community.

SACRED PLACES

The Incas' sacred places were buildings—like temples, plazas, alters, and shrines—or natural settings where people would make contact with the *huacas*. Some chroniclers, like Bernabé Cobo, listed as many as 328 of them around Cuzco.

PRIESTS

In charge of the rituals, celebrations, offerings, and sacrifices required to be made to each god or *huaca*, they also interpreted divine commands and relayed them to the community. At the head of all priests in the empire was the High Priest of the Sun or Willaq Umu.

THE WORLD IN MINIATURE

Conopas are miniature plants and animals, usually made out of stone. The Incas considered them sacred and believed they embodied their livestock and crops. To ask for fertility or abundance of something, they would make offerings to its *conopa*.

YOU'RE INVITED TO MY PARTY

Would you go to a party with a mummy? If you lived in the time of the Incas, of course you would! It was totally normal for the *mallquis* to participate in celebrations and processions. Part of the ritual was to light a fire in front of the mummy and toss his food and *chicha* (corn beer) into it.

Art and Beliefs

The Incas passed down their worldview and way of life via stories, rituals, and images. Imperial artists and artisans created abstract geometric designs with mysterious meanings and depicted some of the plants and animals that inhabit the Andean landscape. Unlike other groups—like the Moche or the Nazca—the Incas didn't depict people or gods; instead, they produced symbols that were so simple and easy to recognize that they became a sign of Incan presence. These designs were used to decorate different objects, above all those given as gifts to the lords of different regions and those used by the Incan nobility.

Their creations weren't pieces of art like we think of today but rather objects designed to accomplish important tasks. Their formal beauty was related to their function, either as a sign of prestige, a ritual object, or a mark of authority. Furthermore, their art was in service to the government: it was used to communicate ideas that organized the social, economic, and political life of all Tahuantinsuyo. To this end, they created an imperial style, which incorporated elements of very old traditions and beliefs that were shared by various groups in the Andes. These symbols and their meanings made it possible to exchange ideas and helped spread the Incas' world view.

IS IT ART?

Maybe you're asking yourself if the Incas really had artists like we do today, if they made art for pleasure and not just to fulfill a particular purpose. It's hard to understand the Incas' artwork because every society develops its own forms of representation and kinds of creative expression. Since the beginning of time, art has been a reflection of the time and place in which the artist grew up and developed. That's why works of art help us understand the cultures in which they were created.

TOCAPUS
These geometric designs inside of little squares decorated clothing and *quero* (wooden cups). Researchers believe that each *tocapu* has its own meaning, conveying a vast array of ideas ranging from regions and places to military ranks and religious symbols.

The Art of Weaving

Do you know what gift an Inca most appreciated? It wasn't an object of silver or gold. Can you guess what they wanted? Finely woven and decorated fabric! That's why making textiles was one of the most important activities in Tahuantinsuyo. In their homes people wove garments and everyday things—like clothing, blankets, bags, and string—but in the royal workshops they produced fine textiles that were used by nobility, the army, and religious officials.

Those in charge of spinning and weaving for the Incan government were the *acllas*, women chosen at a young age whose lives were totally dedicated to making the highest quality woolens and cloths. Alongside them, the most sophisticated weavers—or master weavers—were the *cumbicamayocs*. Both groups produced the most luxurious fabrics, known as *cumbis*.

The imperial warehouses were always well stocked with all kinds of textiles. The rulers of Cuzco provided uniforms and clothing for the members of their army, while the finest tunics or *uncu* were used to establish and reinforce alliances with the leaders of each community.

Textiles also had great religious importance. Intricate cloths have been found in sacred places, and researchers believe that they were used as offerings. Finally, fabrics played a central role in the daily life of the empire because clothing—like accessories—signaled the wearer's rank and social position. This relationship between people and their clothing is part of an ancestral tradition that began developing in the Andes more than 5,000 years ago.

PLANT, GROW, WEAVE
Old and young all participated in the creation of textiles in some way. The smallest could collect flowers, roots, berries, and feathers, which would be used to dye the fibers or decorate the fabrics. Grown-ups were in charge of growing the plants that would be used as natural dyes and raising the animals that would provide different kinds of wool. Spinning and weaving were jobs done mostly by women.

SEWING BASKETS
Many artifacts have been discovered in baskets like this, which date back to Incan times: needles made of animal bone and metal; spinning tools of stone, clay, and wood; as well as balls of wool and cotton.

INCAN STYLE

THE MEN AND WOMEN OF TAHUANTINSUYO WORE THE SAME GARMENTS AS THE INCAN RULER AND THE COYA, BUT WITH A MUCH SIMPLER DESIGN AND CRUDER FABRIC.

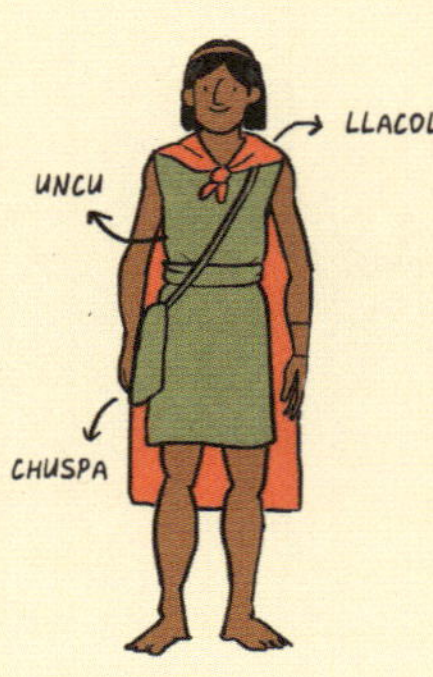

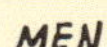

MEN

DRESSED IN A TUNIC OR SHIRT (*UNCU*) AND POSSIBLY A CLOAK WORN OVER THE SHOULDERS (*LLACOLLA*), IN ADDITION TO A BAG FOR CARRYING COCA LEAVES (*CHUSPA*).

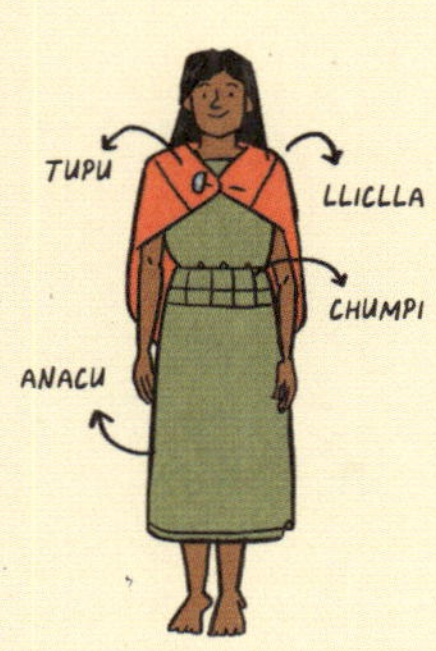

WOMEN

WORE A WRAP DRESS FASTENED AT THE SHOULDER (*ANACU*), WITH A SASH (*CHUMPI*) AROUND THE WAIST, IN ADDITION TO A CLOAK (*LLICLLA*), WHICH WAS DRAPED OVER THE SHOULDERS AND FASTENED ON THE CHEST WITH A PIN (*TUPU*).

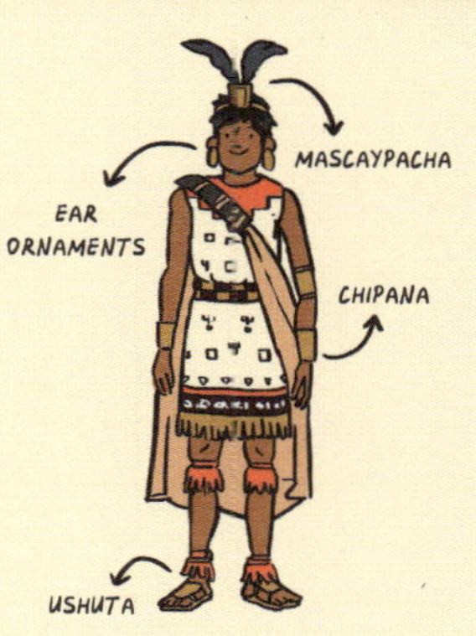

THE INCA

DRESSED IN THE FINEST *UNCU* BEARING THE EMBLEMS OF HIS SOCIAL GROUP OR *PANACA*, IN ADDITION TO OTHER ACCESSORIES THAT SYMBOLIZED HIS POWER, LIKE EAR ORNAMENTS, *CHIPANAS*, AND ESPECIALLY THE *MASCAYPACHA*.

THE COYA

ALSO DRESSED WITH THE SYMBOLS OF HER OWN NOBLE LINEAGE, IN ADDITION TO ELABORATE *TUPUS* OF FINE METAL AND JEWELRY DECORATED WITH *SPONDYLUS* SHELLS AND PRECIOUS STONES.

WEAVERS OF TAQUILE

TAQUILE ISLAND

ON THIS ISLAND IN LAKE TITICACA, THE WEAVING TRADITION DATES BACK TO THE ANCIENT INCA, PUCARÁ AND COLLA CIVILIZATIONS. ALTHOUGH THEIR TEXTILE ART DESIGNS INCORPORATE NEW SYMBOLS AND IMAGES, THEY STILL KEEP TO THE STYLE AND TECHNIQUES INHERITED FROM PRE-HISPANIC CULTURES.

NATURAL AND ORGANIC
Did you know the Incas used natural materials to dye the threads for their textiles? They got orange from annatto or achiote seeds; shades of blue from indigo; the color black from tara seeds; and yellow from the pepper tree. For red, they used the cochineal, a small insect that lives as a parasite in the prickly-pear cactus.

All That Glitters Is (Not) Gold...

Imagine a building so luxurious that its walls are covered in plates of gold. Its courtyards have life-sized statues of men, women, and children, as well as plants and animals, all made out of gold and silver. And everything, from the pots and containers to the tools, is made of precious metals. According to the chronicler Garcilaso de la Vega, these were the dazzling riches housed within Coricancha or the Temple of the Sun, one of the principal structures of Tahuantinsuyo. Upon their arrival in the Andes, the Spanish were so impressed by the number of luxurious objects they found there and elsewhere that they worked up a fever for treasure hunting.

For the Incas, in contrast, precious metals had other purposes: beyond being just accessories or luxuries, they symbolized what was sacred. As in the case of textiles, metal statues and tools were given as gifts between high dignitaries and, more importantly, as offerings to the *huacas**. Most of the gold and silver pieces that have been preserved are small metal statues (idols) that are lavishly dressed and were used in rituals. And because Incan celebrations and rites always had *chicha* (corn beer) and something to carry and serve it in, the imperial metalsmiths also made gold and silver cups called *aquillas.*

More than 1,000 years before Tahuantinsuyo existed, various Andean communities were already experts at metalwork. The Incas didn't develop new technologies but rather took advantage of the metallurgic traditions of other groups (like the Chimu on the northern coast and the Ychsmas on the central coast). They organized a large group of metalsmiths who created different objects—not just fine pieces of gold and silver but also weapons for their army and copper and bronze tools for their people's daily use.

*Forgot what this means? Look in the glossary at the back of the book!

1. Communities under Incan control provided labor for work in the mines.

2. After being extracted, the minerals were processed using a stone mill to separate the metal (ore) from the waste rock (gangue).

3. The metal was smelted in furnaces in well-ventilated locations.

RELICS OF THE PAST
Many gold and silver pieces produced by the Incas were melted down or sent to Spain after the invasion. These small metal statues, dressed in miniature clothing, survive today because they were buried as part of rituals and offerings.

TECHNIQUES AND TOOLS
In order to decorate their metal pieces, ancient Peruvians used techniques like embossing, openwork, and filigree. To do so, they used tools like chisels, gravers, and burins.

4.
Various metalsmithing techniques were used to shape the objects, for example lamination, in which an ingot is flattened into a metal sheet using a hammer. Handheld hammers made of basalt or andesite were the most commonly used tools.

The Incan Army

If you were in charge of a powerful empire, how big would your army be? Maybe so big that when your enemies saw it, they would prefer to be your allies. That's how it was with the Incan army, which grew over the course of several generations through military campaigns to expand Tahuantinsuyo. The rulers prepared everything ahead of time so they could set off with as many warriors as possible as well as an entire entourage to build roads and bridges ahead of their advance.

During the first military campaigns, some groups agreed to or even sought to ally themselves with the Incas so that the army would protect them from their rivals. Groups that joined Tahuantinsuyo were required to enlist their own troops; as such, members of diverse communities became part of the increasingly large Incan army.

While serving in the military, warriors received food and clothing from the state. Because the troops were made up of men from different groups, who each had their own responsibilities, they didn't have to serve for very long, and they also took a break from fighting during harvest times.

Over time, being a member of the Incan army became a way for noblemen to distinguish themselves. In the decades before the Spanish invasion, campaigns of reconquest (when a new Inca ascended to power, he had to reconquer all of the groups who had been subjected by his predecessors) became more difficult. For this reason, troops became specialized: large armies of farmers and shepherds were replaced by warriors from groups like the Chachapoyas and the Cañaris, who were dedicated exclusively to fighting. These soldiers became veteran experts who learned fierce tactics for facing off against groups that resisted domination.

INCAN DIPLOMACY
Military force wasn't the only or even the principal strategy employed by the Incas in their expansion campaigns. Unlike other empires, giving gifts and proposing alliances were important parts of the conquering process.

THE INCAS' WEAPONS
Slingshots and bolas were often used to attack an enemy from a short distance away, but then the armies would fight hand-to-hand. At this close range, the Incas' primary weapon was the mace.
Sling or slingshot made of wool or braided fiber.
Axe made of stone or copper sheets.
1
2
3
Bolas with two or three round stones attached to a cord. It would be hurled at the opponent's neck, arms, or legs.
Padded cotton shirts to protect the body.
Wooden shield and helmet lined with cloth.
MACE
Made of a round or star-shaped head of stone or metal, with a wooden handle fitted through a hole in the middle.
It usually had six points.
Between 12 and 24 in.
6 in.
Stone, copper, or bronze.
HOW ELEGANT!
SOME CHRONICLES DESCRIBE THE SOLDIERS OF THE IMPERIAL ARMY WEARING BEAUTIFUL TUNICS WITH A BLACK-AND-WHITE CHECKERED PATTERN.

Qhapaq Ñan: The Great Inca Road

Qhapaq Ñan is a large network of roads, more than twenty thousand miles long, that runs through the current territories of six South American countries: Colombia, Ecuador, Bolivia, Chile, Argentina, and Peru. The Incas extended roads built by other states—like Wari, Chimu, and Tiwanaku—to build the most important and efficient public works project in the pre-Hispanic world. According to the Spanish chronicler Bernabé Cobo, a package sent from Cuzco to Lima during the colonial period would take twelve days to arrive at its destination on horseback but only three days if it traveled in the hands of the *chasquis* or Incan messengers. Totally incredible!

Different materials and techniques were used to build roads on the sandy coasts, on the rocky peaks of the puna (high plateau), in the dense forests of the jungle, and in the mountain valleys. In these conditions, riding on an animal or in a cart was much harder than going by foot. This led to the success of the *chasquis,* who traversed the Qhapaq Ñan using an efficient system of relays (similar to staging posts!).

This great road was only used for state matters: *chasquis* carried official messages; llama caravans transported food and resources, like maize, potatoes, and cotton; soldiers marched toward their next position; and even rulers with their entourages traveled along its trails and over its bridges. By connecting the empire's four *suyos* or regions, the Qhapaq Ñan gave its residents access to different terrains and resources. Today, this monumental work of Incan engineering lives on. Residents of the Andes work along and are connected by its ancient routes, helping to preserve and restore its legacy. By travelling these roads, which have become an important tourist attraction, you can learn about the history and culture of Peru.

A BRIDGE FOR EVERY ROUTE

The Incas' skill for adapting to the Andean territory—and to the needs of each of its communities—is evident in their construction of different kinds of bridges. Across the length of their great road network, they made bridges of rope, wood, and stone, according to the resources and conditions of the landscape. One of these bridges is called Queshuachaca (located in Canas, Cuzco), and it is periodically restored even today.

FAST AND FURIOUS

The *chasquis* traveled between six and nine miles before arriving at a little house called a *chasquihuasi*, where another *chasqui* waited to run the next segment of the road. As soon as the runner was seen approaching, a conch-shell trumpet or *pututu* was blown to let his companion know to get ready. In this way, twenty-five *chasquis* could cover between 150 and 225 miles in a single day (depending on which route they chose). So orders sent from Quito would have gotten to Cuzco in about a week.

TAMBOS TO BETTER SERVE YOU

Tambos were places where travelers could rest and resupply along their way to distant communities and administrative centers.

Great Structures

In deep valleys, on icy hilltops, and even in one of the world's driest deserts, the Incas built administrative centers, way stations, fortresses, estates, palaces, and shrines. As they expanded across the entire Andean mountain range, they encountered different natural regions. How did they manage to build on so many different terrains?

The Incas developed their own architectural style, easy to recognize and reproduce: the majority of their buildings have a single story and just one rectangular room. The doors and windows have a trapezoidal shape, which is to say they are wider on the bottom and narrower at the top. The roofs are bulky and made of thatch. And the walls are not perpendicular to the floor but rather slanted inward.

As the empire was growing, the Incas' new power showed in their buildings. Temples allowed them to spread the sun cult to the provinces, while *tambos* gave officials a place to stay as they traveled along the Qhapaq Ñan. Places like Huanucopampa and Tomebamba were home to thousands of people who had relocated from distant regions in order to serve the state.

As if they were puzzle pieces or building blocks, stones of every size were carved and put together very precisely to build impressive walls. These are the most famous example of the great variety of techniques and materials that the Incas used across Tahuantinsuyo. To understand the relationship these great structures had with their environment, you have to look at the landscape that surrounds them.

KINDS OF STRUCTURES
The majority of the *callancas*, *canchas*, and *colcas* were simple buildings that could be adapted to serve different purposes. For example, the *callancas* (1) were large rectangular buildings with various entrances and doorways, which served as lodging for officials, among other things. The *cancha* (2) was a courtyard or central plaza surrounded by buildings that may have been houses and workshops for the production of goods. The *colcas* (3) were storehouses. An *ushnu* (4) was a structure shaped like a truncated pyramid or platform that the Inca used for public ceremonies and rituals.

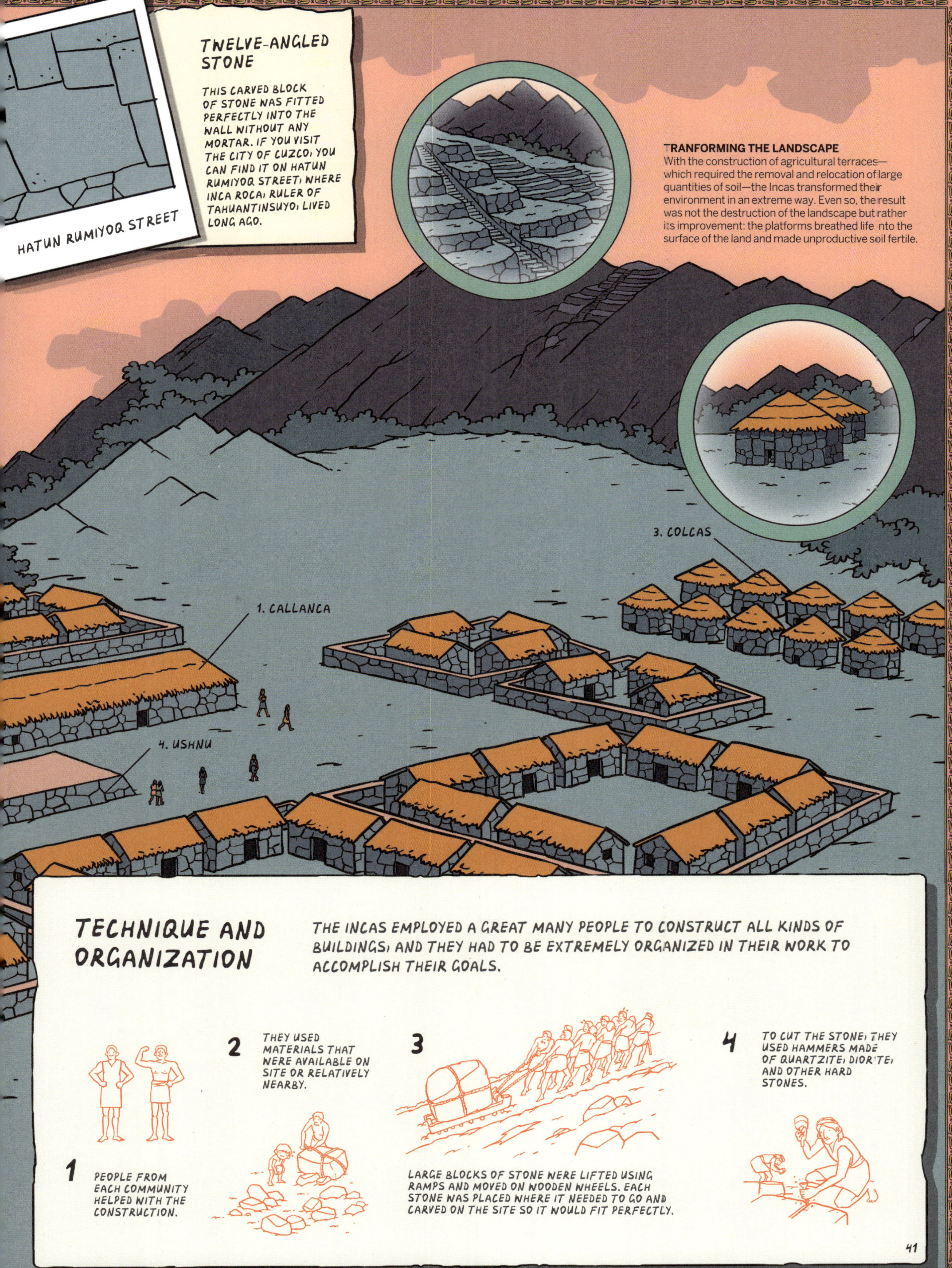
HATUN RUMIYOQ STREET
TWELVE-ANGLED STONE
THIS CARVED BLOCK OF STONE WAS FITTED PERFECTLY INTO THE WALL WITHOUT ANY MORTAR. IF YOU VISIT THE CITY OF CUZCO, YOU CAN FIND IT ON HATUN RUMIYOQ STREET, WHERE INCA ROCA, RULER OF TAHUANTINSUYO, LIVED LONG AGO.
TRANFORMING THE LANDSCAPE
With the construction of agricultural terraces—which required the removal and relocation of large quantities of soil—the Incas transformed their environment in an extreme way. Even so, the result was not the destruction of the landscape but rather its improvement: the platforms breathed life into the surface of the land and made unproductive soil fertile.
3. COLCAS
1. CALLANCA
4. USHNU
TECHNIQUE AND ORGANIZATION
THE INCAS EMPLOYED A GREAT MANY PEOPLE TO CONSTRUCT ALL KINDS OF BUILDINGS, AND THEY HAD TO BE EXTREMELY ORGANIZED IN THEIR WORK TO ACCOMPLISH THEIR GOALS.
1
PEOPLE FROM EACH COMMUNITY HELPED WITH THE CONSTRUCTION.
2
THEY USED MATERIALS THAT WERE AVAILABLE ON SITE OR RELATIVELY NEARBY.
3
LARGE BLOCKS OF STONE WERE LIFTED USING RAMPS AND MOVED ON WOODEN WHEELS. EACH STONE WAS PLACED WHERE IT NEEDED TO GO AND CARVED ON THE SITE SO IT WOULD FIT PERFECTLY.
4
TO CUT THE STONE, THEY USED HAMMERS MADE OF QUARTZITE, DIORITE, AND OTHER HARD STONES.
41

The Stone of Sayhuite

On top of a stepped pyramid, inside an ancient Incan place of worship, you will find this massive carved stone with mysterious significance. On its surface, buildings, platforms, and irrigation canals have been carved alongside mountains, rivers, and lakes. Men and women live in this miniature world and share it with pumas, llamas, snakes, toads, lizards, condors, monkeys, and crabs. This monolith's purpose is still unknown, but it seems to be a great *paccha* or fountain: when it rained, water would pool in the hollows of the rock and flow along its surface, eventually coming out through small holes and watering the land.

The stone of Sayhuite forms part of the Concacha archaeological complex, where it is believed that the Incas worshiped water. It's considered a one-of-a-kind *huaca* or shrine: unlike other *huacas* made out of stone by the Incas, this one has more than two hundred figures carved in great detail. The monolith is surrounded by altars and is near a structure that looks like a labyrinth. It was certainly a very important religious site: some researchers think it might have been an oracle!

Everyone who visits the Curahuasi (Apurímac) district to admire the stone tries to decipher its meaning. Maybe it was a sacred altar devoted to the water, a symbol of the rains that irrigated fields and benefited crops. It might also have been a territorial marker that signaled the division between two historically competing groups: the Incas, from Cuzco, and the Chancas, who were conquered early on. Or perhaps it is a map of Tahuantinsuyo, with its many regions and climates. Whatever Sayhuite may have been in the past, today it is an example of the ancient Peruvians' skill and artistry. Would you like to discover its meaning?

Llamas and alpacas seem to be grazing in the valley.

* Four cats mark the four cardinal points.

Figures of men and women, shown in pairs, can be made out near the rivers and lakes. The woman is carrying a jug of water.

A TOAST TO NATURE
The Incas had a special relationship with their environment, and it was common to "toast" the river as a way of saying thanks. To do so, they used vessels with small spouts, called *pacchas*. When they put water or *chicha* (corn beer) into one of these vessels, the liquid would flow through it and come out through the spout.

Reservoirs collect the water that arrives from the upper part.

ANCIENT PERUVIAN ORACLES

ORACLES WERE SACRED PLACES WHERE PEOPLE—AND COMMUNITY LEADERS—WOULD GO ON PILGRIMAGES TO CONSULT A DEITY AND GET ANSWERS. AMONG THE MAIN ORACLES OF ANCIENT PERU, SOME NOTABLE ONES ARE PACHACAMAC, IN LIMA; TITICACA, ON THE ISLAND OF THE SUN; AND CATEQUIL, VERY CLOSE TO HUAMACHUCO.

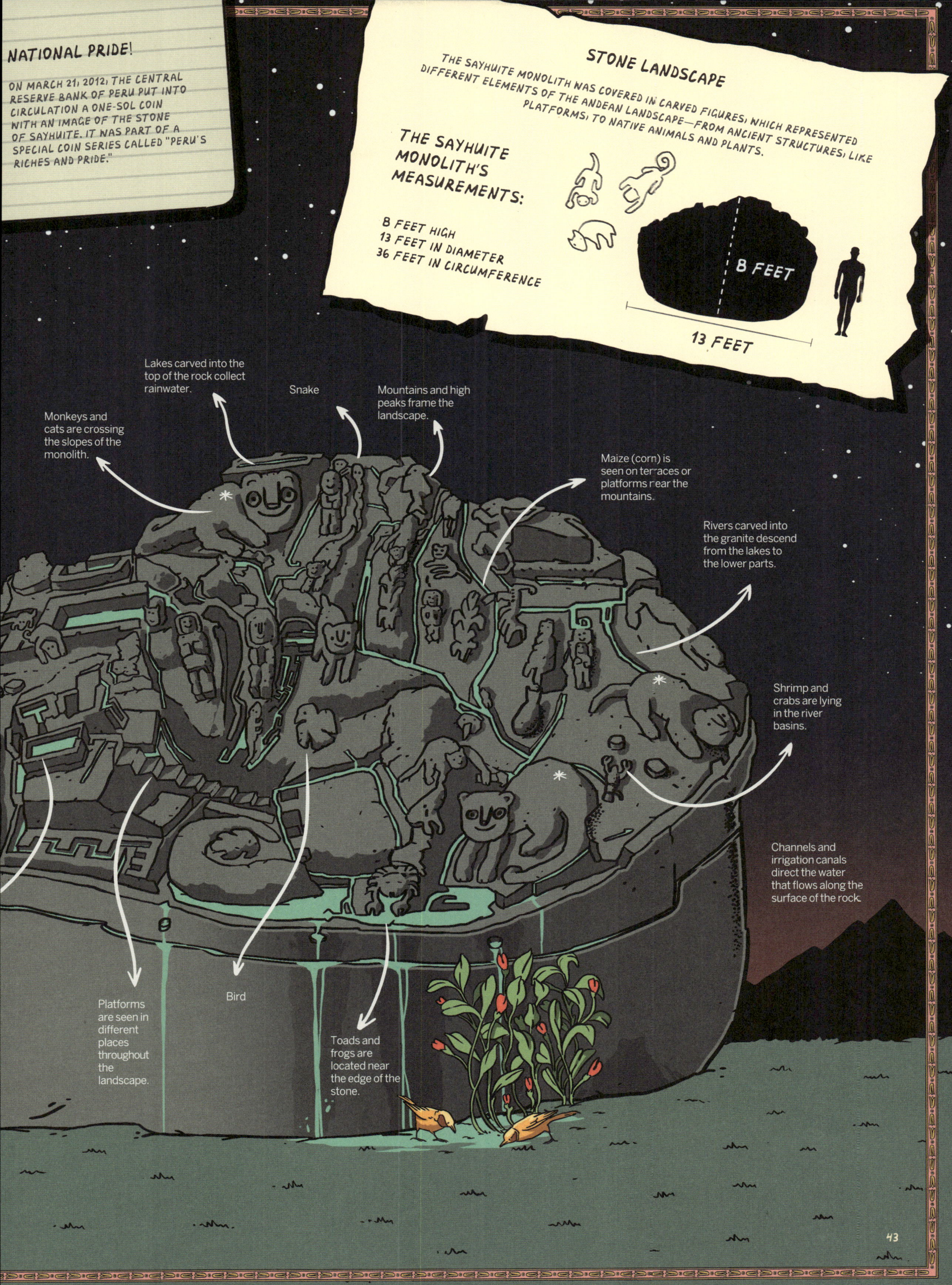

NATIONAL PRIDE!
ON MARCH 21, 2012, THE CENTRAL RESERVE BANK OF PERU PUT INTO CIRCULATION A ONE-SOL COIN WITH AN IMAGE OF THE STONE OF SAYHUITE. IT WAS PART OF A SPECIAL COIN SERIES CALLED "PERU'S RICHES AND PRIDE."
STONE LANDSCAPE
THE SAYHUITE MONOLITH WAS COVERED IN CARVED FIGURES, WHICH REPRESENTED DIFFERENT ELEMENTS OF THE ANDEAN LANDSCAPE—FROM ANCIENT STRUCTURES, LIKE PLATFORMS, TO NATIVE ANIMALS AND PLANTS.
THE SAYHUITE MONOLITH'S MEASUREMENTS:
8 FEET HIGH
13 FEET IN DIAMETER
36 FEET IN CIRCUMFERENCE
8 FEET
13 FEET
Lakes carved into the top of the rock collect rainwater.
Snake
Mountains and high peaks frame the landscape.
Monkeys and cats are crossing the slopes of the monolith.
Maize (corn) is seen on terraces or platforms near the mountains.
Rivers carved into the granite descend from the lakes to the lower parts.
Shrimp and crabs are lying in the river basins.
Channels and irrigation canals direct the water that flows along the surface of the rock.
Platforms are seen in different places throughout the landscape.
Bird
Toads and frogs are located near the edge of the stone.

Incan Palaces and Royal Estates

From Huiracocha to Huascar, the great rulers of the Incan Empire built impressive, luxurious properties. After defeating first the Cuyos and then the Tambos (see pages 16–17), Pachacuti put up estates and palaces in Pisac and Ollantaytambo. They were built to commemorate and record the triumph of each conquest but also as a way of organizing the recently conquered populations. Their facilities were designed for the comfort of the Inca's *panaca* or family group, as well as to elevate his reputation and—later on—to uphold the cult of his mummy. It was each ruler's duty to found a *panaca* and build an estate. Can you even imagine what these remarkable structures must have been like when the Incas ruled the Andes?

The royal estates were useful and also beautiful. The territory they encompassed included lakes, palaces, and farmland. Many included entire villages whose residents worked in service to the Inca. They had sacred sites but also recreational spaces where the nobles would hunt, raise birds, and garden. They were located in strategic locations that were important to the local populations and ideal for producing various goods, like maize, pepper, coca, gold, salt, and wood. No obstacle was too great when it came to building these properties: it's said that the Inca Huayna Capac had the river moved from one side of the valley to the other when he built his residence at Yucay.

When visiting these estates today, you can admire not only their beauty but also their significance: in their construction and design, each ruler expressed his values, his history, and his way of understanding the world.

LIFE IN CHINCHERO
Topa Inca Yupanqui's palace was located on this estate, where the ruler would go to relax for as long as he needed. He would be accompanied by some of his wives as well as by other noblemen.

MACHU PICCHU
OLLANTAYTAMBO
YUCAY
CALCA
CHINCHERO
HUCHUY QOSQO
PÍSAC
TIPÓN
MUNA
★ CUZCO
ROYAL TERRITORIES
EACH OF THE ESTATES AND PALACES CORRESPONDS TO AN INCAN RULER AND HIS PARTICULAR STYLE. HOWEVER, SOME OF THESE BUILDINGS WERE COMPLETED—OR RECONSTRUCTED—DURING DIFFERENT PERIODS THROUGHOUT THE HISTORY OF TAHUANTINSUYO.
BUILT BY HUIRACOCHA INCA (BEFORE 1438)
BUILT BY PACHACUTI (1438–1471)
BUILT BY TOPA INCA YUPANQUI (1471–1493)
BUILT BY HUAYNA CAPAC (1493–1525)
BUILT BY HUASCAR (1525–1532)
THE POWER OF THE *PANACAS*
The Cuzco nobility was made up of families who were descendants of previous Incan rulers. These families were the *panacas*. When the Incan ruler died, his *panaca* was no longer at the height of political power, but as long as they worshiped his mummy—who continued "living" in his palace—they kept their property and their privilege.
CHINCHERO ARCHAEOLOGICAL CENTER
(If you're ever in Cuzco, you can go see it!)
HOW IT WAS BUILT
To build Chinchero, Topa Inca Yupanqui recruited a workforce from all over the empire. He ordered his men to gather chiefs and their people from all of his lands and bring them to the city of Cuzco. According to the chronicler Betanzos, 20,000 people showed up!
LUCKY MUMMY
In spite of their luxury and comfort, it's thought that the rulers didn't spend much time in their palaces. Oddly enough, they were actually meant to be permanent residences for their mummies.

Machu Picchu!

Can you guess which is the most famous Incan residence in the world? Machu Picchu! This estate belonged to Pachacuti, celebrated ruler of Tahuantinsuyo, who made the Incan State into one of history's largest empires. The impressive stone structure, considered one of the New Seven Wonders of the World, is located at approximately eight thousand feet above sea level, on a rocky ledge between the hills of Huayna Picchu and Machu Picchu, from which it gets its name. Today, Machu Picchu—"old mountain" in Quechua—is one of Peru's main tourist attractions, but to the Andean people six hundred years ago, it was the epitome of a landscape transformed in harmony with nature.

It took many people and significant effort for the Incas to build this magnificent estate, which appears to emerge naturally from the mountains. It was a difficult adventure for Pachacuti and his men to get to the edge of the jungle where it is located, a land they knew to be dangerous and filled with ferocious beasts. The area was wild and steep, with deep, swiftly moving rivers, but it also offered important resources like wood and mines rich in silver and gold. Furthermore, it had the right climate for producing coca, an essential leaf for rituals.

Life in Machu Picchu was calm and pleasant because it was a place of rest for the Inca. Temples, fountains, terraces, workshops, and a solar observatory also indicate the presence of priests, farmers, and artisans. In this sacred space, located between the Andes and the Amazon, the spirit and grandeur of the Incan Empire are present even today.

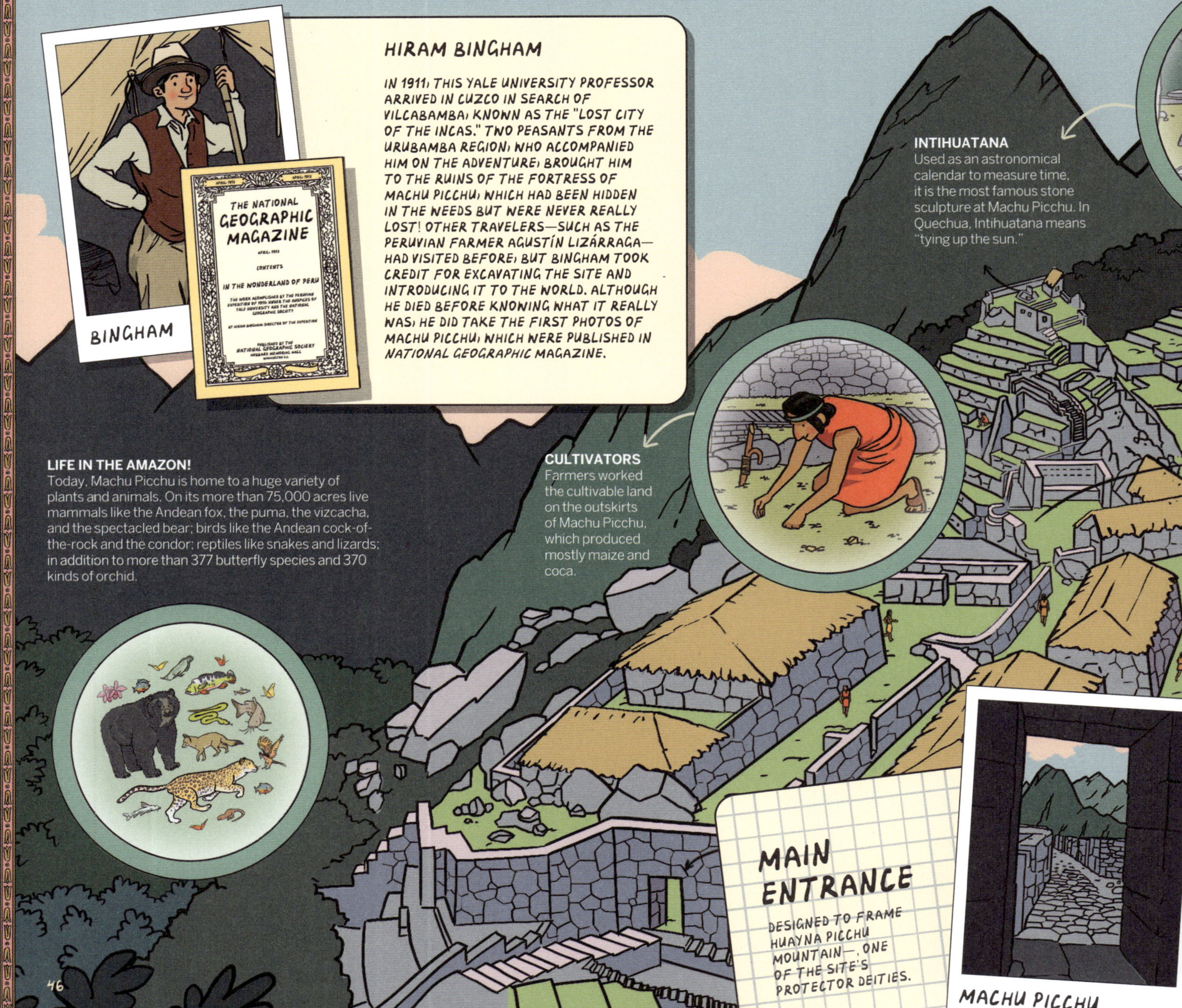

WORLD HERITAGE SITE
IN 1983, MACHU PICCHU WAS DECLARED A UNESCO WORLD HERITAGE SITE, A RECOGNITION BESTOWED ON PLACES WITH CULTURAL OR NATURAL IMPORTANCE, WHICH ARE CONSIDERED THE JOINT LEGACY OF ALL THE WORLD'S PEOPLE.
5 PERÚ
SOLES
1983 MACHU PICCHU
WORLD HERITAGE SITE
SACRED ROCK
Shaped like Yanantin, the mountain found behind it in the landscape, this rock may have been aligned for the study of celestial bodies.
ROYAL FAMILY
Members of the Inca's *panaca* were temporary residents of Machu Picchu and were in charge of worshiping the Inca's mummy.
BETWEEN HEAVEN AND EARTH
Machu Picchu had a permanent population of about five hundred residents, whose labor was organized into two major sectors: the *hanan* (or high part) and the *urin* (or low part). For the Incas, the world was divided into these two opposite planes, which were different yet complementary.
SACRED PLAZA
Here we find the Main Temple and the Temple of the Three Windows. In this plaza, reunions, parties, and rituals were celebrated.
IF THIS IS THE PALACE, JUST IMAGINE THE ESTATE!
SOME RESEARCHERS BELIEVE THAT MACHU PICCHU IS NOTHING MORE THAN THE MAIN PALACE OF AN EXTRAORDINARY ESTATE BELONGING TO PACHACUTI, WHICH INCLUDES MANY OTHER RELATED PROPERTIES.
?
?
?
HOUSE OF THE INCA
Temporary residence of Pachacuti or his representative, it is strategically located with direct connections to the freshest water fountains and the Temple of the Sun.
TEMPLE OF THE CONDOR
Housed inside is a great rock in the shape of a condor, an Andean bird that symbolized power and fertility.
TEMPLE OF THE SUN
A sacred enclosure only accessible to priests and members of the nobility, it was dedicated to the worship and adoration of the sun god.
CEREMONIAL FOUNTAINS
There are a total of sixteen fountains located in the urban area of Machu Picchu.

How Did the Spanish Get to Peru?

At the end of the 15th century, in the Kingdom of Spain, a Genoese sailor named Christopher Columbus was hired by the king and queen to find a new route to the East Indies. He crossed the Atlantic Ocean as planned—but he arrived at a group of islands that weren't on any map! To everyone's surprise, the archipelago was part of what we now call America, a continent the Europeans didn't even know existed.

After Columbus arrived in 1492, other sailors and adventurers also came to these shores in search of fame and fortune. At that time, crossing large oceans was a task filled with danger. Despite the scientific and technological advances taking place in Europe, maps were still unreliable, no one knew how many continents there were or where they were located, and people imagined that beyond the known territories lived terrible beasts and fantastic beings.

One of these adventurers was the Spaniard Francisco Pizarro, a veteran soldier and admirer of Columbus. When he was in Panama, after the discovery of the Southern Ocean—now called the Pacific—he heard about a kingdom of infinite riches called Birú (Peru). He joined up with two other Spaniards—the soldier Diego de Almagro and the priest Hernando de Luque—and they formed a company to find and conquer it.

On November 14, 1524, Pizarro left on his first voyage aboard the ship *Santiago*. He didn't know it then, but two more journeys and several complications awaited him before he would accomplish his goal. Eight years later, after many sacrifices, he finally made it to the Incan Empire.

PIZARRO'S VOYAGES
IN SEARCH OF A KINGDOM OF INCALCULABLE RICHES SOUTH OF PANAMA, PIZARRO EMBARKED ON THE ADVENTURE THAT WOULD LEAD HIM TO THE INCAN EMPIRE.
FIRST VOYAGE
I
1524-1525 PIZARRO AND HIS MEN DISEMBARK AT PUERTO PIÑAS (COLOMBIA), BUT THEY DON'T FIND ANY GOLD. THEY CONTINUE ON THEIR WAY AND ARRIVE AT SAN TELMO, PUERTO ESPERANZA, AND RÍO DE LA ESPERA. THE NATIVE PEOPLE OF THE COAST ATTACK THEM, LEAVING SOME DEAD AND WOUNDED. ALMAGRO GOES IN SEARCH OF REINFORCEMENTS, AND THE OTHERS REMAIN WAITING.
BIG CHANGES
EUROPEAN CURIOSITY WAS FUELED BY STORIES AND NOVELTIES BROUGHT HOME BY THE GREAT EXPEDITIONS. ANIMALS LIKE LLAMAS AND FOODS LIKE CACAO—BROUGHT FROM FAR-AWAY, UNKNOWN LANDS—ARRIVED FOR THE FIRST TIME IN THE OLD WORLD. DURING THAT PERIOD, ASTONISHING SCIENTIFIC DISCOVERIES, LIKE THE LAW OF GRAVITY, WERE ALSO BEING MADE, AND SEVERAL NEW CHEMICAL ELEMENTS CAME TO LIGHT. (SEE PAGES 6–7.)
II
1526-1527 REINFORCEMENTS ARRIVE, AND THEY SET SAIL WITH APPROXIMATELY 110 SOLDIERS. THEY GO BACK AND BURN DOWN THE HOMES OF THE NATIVE PEOPLE WHO ATTACKED THEM. HAVING FOUND NO GOLD, THEY RECEIVE ORDERS TO END THE EXPEDITION. ON THE ISLA DEL GALLO, ONLY 13 MEN DECIDE TO STAY WITH PIZARRO AND CONTINUE THEIR VOYAGE: THE REST LEAVE. THEY ARRIVE AT TUMBES AND FIND EVIDENCE OF A GREAT EMPIRE: THE REGION OF THE CHIMU HAD BOTH CIVILIZATION AND RICHES. PIZARRO RETURNS TO SPAIN AND REQUESTS THE CROWN'S PROTECTION TO BEGIN HIS CONQUEST.
SECOND VOYAGE
FIRST ENCOUNTERS
IN 1526, HAVING BEEN SENT BY FRANCISCO PIZARRO ON AN EXPLORATORY EXPEDITION TO THE SOUTH, BARTOLOMÉ RUIZ SPOTTED A HUGE RAFT; IT WAS SO BIG THAT HE THOUGHT IT WAS A PORTUGUESE CARAVEL. THE SPANIARDS WERE SHOCKED TO FIND THAT IT WAS MANNED BY INDIGENOUS PEOPLE WHO WERE TRADING VARIOUS PRODUCTS, FROM CAMELID WOOL TO GOLD AND CERAMIC OBJECTS.
CAJAMARCA
CUZCO
PIURA
III
THIRD VOYAGE
1531-1532 THEY SET OFF WITH 180 SOLDIERS AND 37 HORSES. AFTER FINDING GREAT PLUNDER IN THE NORTH OF ECUADOR, SOME SPANIARDS GET SICK WITH WARTS AND DIE. MEANWHILE, REINFORCEMENTS AND ROYAL OFFICIALS ARRIVE AND JOIN THE EXPEDITION. THEY STAY ON THE ISLAND OF PUNÁ FOR FOUR MONTHS, WHERE THEY FIGHT THE INDIGENOUS PEOPLE AND RECEIVE MORE REINFORCEMENTS. THEY ADVANCE AND FIND A ROAD THAT LEADS TO CAJAMARCA AND THUS FINALLY REACH THE INCAN EMPIRE.
49

A FATAL RUMOR
Even though Atahualpa was a prisoner and the empire was in crisis, the Incan army still posed a great threat to the invaders. So when a rumor arrived that an enormous troop was nearing the Spanish encampment to liberate the Inca, Pizarro decided to execute him. Oddly enough, the rumored army never appeared.

WEAPONS OF CONQUEST
When fighting the Incas, the Spanish wore iron armor, carried harquebuses, and were armed with highly destructive canons. But even though gunpowder was crucial in battle, the most valuable "weapons" the invaders had were dogs and, above all, horses.

The Fall of Tahuantinsuyo

What did the arrival of the Spanish mean for the Incan Empire? To begin with, lots of trouble! But the problems actually started much earlier. Viruses and germs that had arrived in Central America with the Europeans turned out to be very contagious and spread rapidly toward the Andean region, becoming deadly epidemics. It's thought that Huayna Capac—who got sick and died in only four days—was one of the first victims. When Pizarro and his men began their invasion of Peru in 1532, thousands of Indigenous people had lost their lives in deadly outbreaks of sicknesses like smallpox and measles.

With the imperial army debilitated by epidemics, it was hard to control discontent in the many different Andean communities that made up Tahuantinsuyo. The Spanish took advantage of this opportunity and allied themselves with groups who opposed the Incas: the Huancas, for example, offered them warriors and provisions and guided them across a land that was unfamiliar to the invading troops.

Meanwhile, the sudden death of Huayna Capac ignited a conflict between his sons Huascar (from Cuzco) and Atahualpa (based in Quito) because both of them wished to rule the empire. This confrontation created tremendous disorder and led to the deaths of hundreds of warriors and Incan military officers. To top it all off, Atahualpa was captured by Pizarro on November 16, 1532. From his cell, he gave orders for his brother to be killed, and in doing so, he pushed those loyal to Huascar into joining the invaders.

Although Atahualpa's capture marked the beginning of the end of Tahuantinsuyo, the Incas went on fighting the Spanish for forty more years. And rebellions—big and small—continued across the entire colony.

BROTHERS AND RIVALS
Fighting did little to serve the brothers who both wished to be the Inca. After Atahualpa ordered Huascar's death, he too was executed by Francisco Pizarro. And, in the end, both sides fell into the hands of the Spanish. It's always best to get along with your family!

ATAHUALPA'S CAPTURE
The Spanish chronicles describing Pizarro's encounter with Atahualpa in the city of Cajamarca are very well known. They tell us that Father Valverde walked up to the Inca and offered him a Bible, a book sacred to the invaders. Atahualpa threw the Bible to the ground and, as a consequence of this rebuff, was taken prisoner. A lesser-known account of what happened that day, which comes from Titu Cusi Yupanqui, nephew of Atahualpa, was told to Brother Marcos García in 1570: before receiving the Bible, the Inca offered the Spanish *aquillas* filled with *chicha*, a drink that was sacred to the Incas. Pizarro's men dumped out the cups without understanding the meaning of such a gesture. This infuriated Atahualpa, who decided in that moment that he too would reject whatever the Spanish offered him.
ATAHUALPA
14th Inca
HUASCAR
13th Inca
HUAYNA CAPAC
12th Inca
GOLD AND SILVER RANSOM
ATAHUALPA, THE CAPTIVE INCA, OFFERED FRANCISCO PIZARRO A ROOM FILLED WITH GOLD AND TWO FILLED WITH SILVER AS A RANSOM TO BUY HIS FREEDOM. IT WAS SENT TO CAJAMARCA FROM ALL OVER TAHUANTINSUYO, AND HE MANAGED TO GATHER AN ENORMOUS FORTUNE, BUT IT COULDN'T PREVENT ATAHUALPA'S DEATH.

Incan Resistance

After the Spanish arrived in Tahuantinsuyo, many things changed in the lives of the empire's residents. Pizarro and his men founded new cities in Piura, Jauja and Cuzco; temples and shrines were looted or destroyed; and the different populations were forced to work for the invaders. Despite this, the children and grandchildren of Huayna Capac tenaciously resisted Spanish domination and the destruction of their culture.

After Huascar's and Atahualpa's deaths, the conquistadores recognized another of their brothers as the new ruler of the empire. His name was Manco Inca, and in the beginning, he got along pretty well with the new arrivals. Pizarro thought it would be easy to control him, but when Manco didn't give him all of the gold he wanted, he ended their alliance. Manco Inca was captured and had to promise his captors more riches in order to escape. Then he organized a great rebellion against the invaders and—according to the chronicler Pedro Pizarro—managed to lay siege to Cuzco with around two-hundred thousand men in 1536.

On one side was the Incan army, and on the other, the Spanish army, which had been joined by thousands of Indigenous groups who were dissatisfied with the Incas. After several months of fighting, the groups loyal to Manco Inca were defeated at Sacsayhuamán.

Nevertheless, the Inca and his followers managed to take refuge in the village of Vilcabamba and continued to resist the Spanish. After Manco Inca's death, his sons Sayri Tupac, Titu Cusi Yupanqui, and Túpac Amaru I were proclaimed Inca—one after another—and they ruled from Vilcabamba for more than forty years. At different moments, they both negotiated with and fought against the conquistadores in an attempt to regain Incan sovereignty. Finally, Túpac Amaru I—the last leader of the Incan resistance—was captured and executed in 1572.

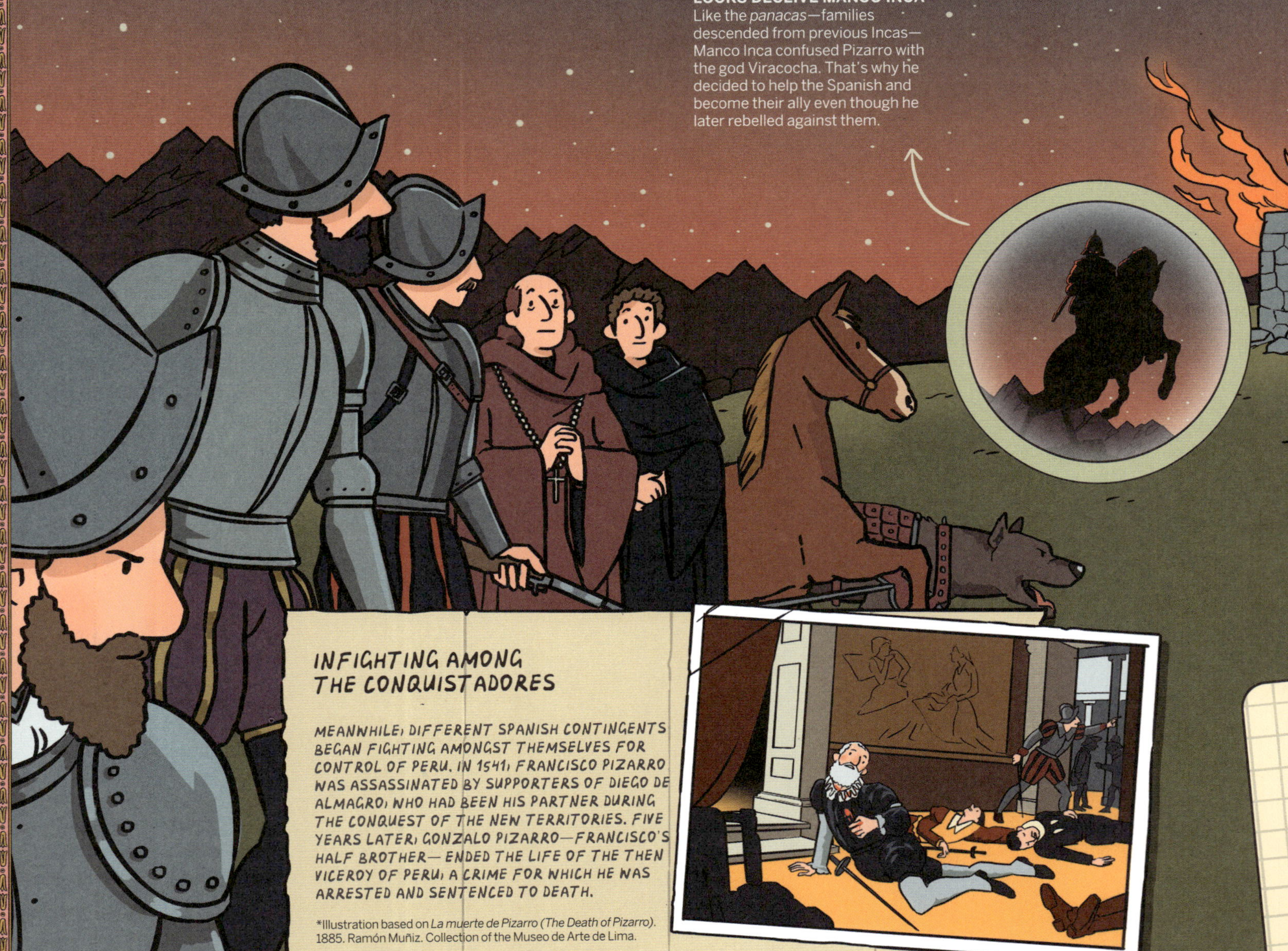

LOOKS DECEIVE MANCO INCA
Like the *panacas*—families descended from previous Incas—Manco Inca confused Pizarro with the god Viracocha. That's why he decided to help the Spanish and become their ally even though he later rebelled against them.

INFIGHTING AMONG THE CONQUISTADORES

MEANWHILE, DIFFERENT SPANISH CONTINGENTS BEGAN FIGHTING AMONGST THEMSELVES FOR CONTROL OF PERU. IN 1541, FRANCISCO PIZARRO WAS ASSASSINATED BY SUPPORTERS OF DIEGO DE ALMAGRO, WHO HAD BEEN HIS PARTNER DURING THE CONQUEST OF THE NEW TERRITORIES. FIVE YEARS LATER, GONZALO PIZARRO—FRANCISCO'S HALF BROTHER—ENDED THE LIFE OF THE THEN VICEROY OF PERU, A CRIME FOR WHICH HE WAS ARRESTED AND SENTENCED TO DEATH.

*Illustration based on *La muerte de Pizarro* (The Death of Pizarro). 1885. Ramón Muñiz. Collection of the Museo de Arte de Lima.

THE VESSEL OF VILCABAMBA
DURING THE ARCHAEOLOGICAL EXCAVATION CARRIED OUT BETWEEN 2009 AND 2010 AT THE SITE OF ESPÍRITU PAMPA, VILCABAMBA, FRAGMENTS OF AN EXTRAORDINARY CERAMIC VESSEL WERE FOUND. A SCENE PAINTED ON THE FRAGMENTS SHOWS THE CONFRONTATION BETWEEN THE SPANISH AND THE INDIGENOUS PEOPLE, COMPLETE WITH THEIR WEAPONS, CLOTHING, AND ANIMALS, AS WELL AS INCAN SYMBOLS. RESEARCHERS WHO HAVE STUDIED IT DON'T BELIEVE IT REPRESENTS A SPECIFIC BATTLE BUT RATHER AN INCAN VISION OF THE FUTURE, ONE IN WHICH THE NATIVE PEOPLE FINALLY MANAGE TO DEFEAT THEIR INVADERS.
*Illustration and references taken from the article *Los fragmentos de Vilcabamba (The Fragments of Vilcabamba)*. Artzi, Nir and Fonseca Santa Cruz. 2019. Drawing: Arturo Rivera Infante.
*Only half of the drawing is seen in this image.
AN IMPENETRABLE REGION
THIS IS HOW MANCO INCA SAW THE VILLAGE OF VILCABAMBA, A WILD AREA IN THE DEEP JUNGLE OF CUZCO. AND THAT'S WHY HE DECIDED TO TAKE REFUGE THERE TO REORGANIZE HIS WARRIORS AND CONTINUE FIGHTING THE INVADERS. AT THE TIME, THE SPANISH STILL HADN'T MANAGED TO ENTER THE REGION.
THE FIERCE, THE BRAVE, THE INCAS
The chroniclers tell us that the army of the Incan resistance fought only on full-moon nights. When they attacked, they let out such terrible battle cries and played their *pututus* (conch-shell trumpets) with such force that they made the earth shake. It also made the Spaniards shake—out of fear!
SILENT RESISTANCE
Although the Spanish enforced the practice of Catholicism and prohibited native religions, thousands of Indigenous settlers continued worshiping their ancestral gods. Neither the destruction of the *huacas* nor the severe punishments given out by the invaders stopped the Indigenous people from finding ways to maintain their religious customs, often in secret.
REBELS AND TRAITORS
AROUND 1544, MANCO INCA GAVE SHELTER TO A GROUP OF SPANIARDS WHO HAD REBELLED AGAINST THE KING OF SPAIN. ALTHOUGH THEY HAD BEEN RECEIVED INTO HIS HOME AND TREATED WELL, THE SPANIARDS GREW TIRED OF THEIR LIFE IN EXILE AND KILLED MANCO IN HOPES THAT IT WOULD WIN THEM A PARDON FROM THE KING.

The Incas According to the Chronicles

From Pizarro's first voyage to the famous Kingdom of Birú (Peru), adventurers, soldiers, and religious men took to writing down all that was happening. At first, the history of the expeditions and the occupation of Incan territory was detailed in the conquistadores' letters. But before long, with so many events to report, books called "chronicles" began being published, which described the Spaniard's exploits and the astonishing things they came across in the Andes.

The first chroniclers to write about the Incas and the conquest of Tahuantinsuyo were European. But, starting at the end of the sixteenth century, Indigenous, Mestizo, and Creole people recorded their own versions of events. Of these, one of the most important was Felipe Guamán Poma de Ayala, whose writings and illustrations explained his ancestors' history, from the origins of the empire all the way to the colonial period. He needed more than a thousand pages to tell it all!

In his *Nueva corónica y buen gobierno (New Chronicle and Good Government)*, Guamán Poma introduces himself as a descendent of Incan nobility and asks the Spanish king to solve the problems facing the Viceroyalty of Peru. He complains about the greed and cruelty of Spanish officials and corrupt priests but also about Mestizos and Indigenous people who abuse their partners. Whether the manuscript ever made it into the hands of the king is a mystery. The work was discovered three hundred years later and published in Paris, France, becoming one of Peru's—and the world's—most important historical documents.

FELIPE GUAMÁN POMA DE AYALA
Born in Huamanga between 1530 and 1550, around the time of the Spanish invasion, he was the son of Guamán Mallqui and Curi Ocllo. According to the chronicler, his father was "*segunda persona del Inca*"—an important political appointment within the Incan hierarchy—and his mother was Huayna Capac's sister. He began writing and illustrating the *New Chronicle* in the final decades of the sixteenth century in hopes of improving the lives of the Andean people.

NEW CHRONICLE AND GOOD GOVERNMENT BY FELIPE GUAMÁN POMA DE AYALA

ILLUSTRATED HISTORY OF THE INCAS BY BROTHER MARTÍN DE MURÚA

ONE HISTORY, TWO CHRONICLERS

BROTHER MARTÍN DE MURÚA WAS A SPANISH PRIEST AND CHRONICLER BORN IN 1540. IN CUZCO, HE HIRED FELIPE GUAMÁN POMA DE AYALA TO ILLUSTRATE HIS BOOK *HISTORIA ILUSTRADA DE LOS INCAS (ILLUSTRATED HISTORY OF THE INCAS)*. BUT GUAMÁN POMA GOT IN AN ARGUMENT WITH MURÚA SOMETIME AROUND 1604 AND DECIDED TO WRITE AND ILLUSTRATE HIS OWN CHRONICLE—WHICH IS WHY THE TWO MEN'S BOOKS ARE SO SIMILAR. IN HIS BOOK, THE ANDEAN CHRONICLER ACCUSES THE SPANIARD OF TREATING THE NATIVE PEOPLE POORLY AND OF LEADING A NOT-SO-CHRISTIAN LIFESTYLE. HE ALSO CRITICIZES THE WAY MURÚA TELLS THE INCAS' STORY.

LOST AND FOUND

UNFORTUNATELY, GUAMÁN POMA DIDN'T LIVE TO SEE HIS WORK'S SUCCESS. THE *NEW CHRONICLE* WAS TOTALLY FORGOTTEN UNTIL 1909, WHEN IT WAS "DISCOVERED" IN THE ROYAL DANISH LIBRARY IN COPENHAGEN (WHERE IT REMAINS TODAY). BUT HOW DID IT END UP THERE? IT IS BELIEVED TO HAVE COME INTO THE HANDS OF CORNELIUS LERCHE, THE DANISH AMBASSADOR TO SPAIN, SOMETIME AROUND 1650 WHEN HE PURCHASED PART OF THE COUNT-DUKE OF OLIVARES'S LIBRARY. IT WAS LOST IN NO TIME!

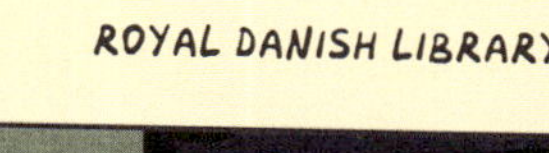
ROYAL DANISH LIBRARY

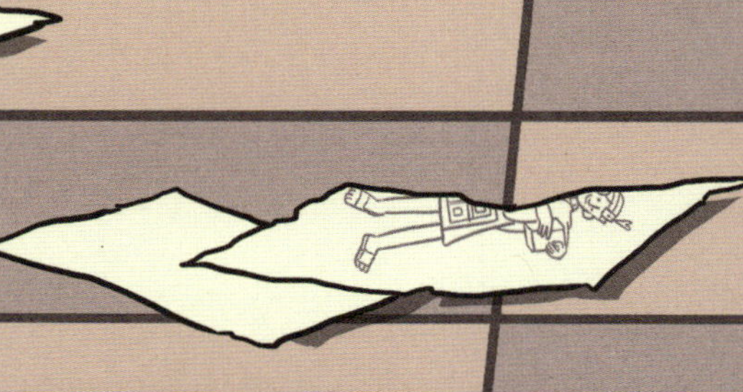

THE ANDEAN CHRONICLER
Author, artist, translator, interpreter, teacher—Guamán Poma was a very talented man! His half brother, the Mestizo priest Martín de Ayala, taught him Spanish, Latin, world history, and also religion. This allowed him to work as an assistant in the Church and an official of the colonial government.
PREGŨTASV. M. RESPOELAV
DONPHELIPE·ELTER
THE INCAS ACCORDING TO GUAMÁN POMA
In his book, Guamán Poma draws on all his knowledge of the world and of European culture. He combines Andean stories with religious teachings and identifies himself as a Christian. Furthermore, he presents a pacifist version of the conquest, in which the Incas—that is to say, his ancestors—do not oppose the Spaniards, but rather submit themselves in good faith. Of course he did hope to deliver his book to the king of Spain, so he used the arguments that would best convince the sovereign to look favorably upon his Peruvian subjects.
FEMALE PROTAGONISTS
Unlike many authors of his time, Guamán Poma was interested in telling the stories of women as well as those of men. In his drawings, he depicts women of the Incan royalty and *acllas* (chosen women), in addition to peasants and workers, young and old.
AN UNEQUAL SOCIETY
DURING THE COLONIAL PERIOD, NOT EVERYONE HAD THE SAME DUTIES OR RIGHTS. THE SPANISH CROWN DIVIDED THE POPULATION INTO TWO LARGE GROUPS: THE "REPUBLIC OF SPANIARDS" (FORMED BY THOSE BORN IN SPAIN AND THEIR DESCENDANTS) AND THE "REPUBLIC OF INDIANS" (COMPOSED OF THE NATIVE POPULATION). THE NEW ORDER WAS VERY UNEQUAL! HOWEVER, IT WAS NEVER VERY RIGID, AND MANY PEOPLE MANAGED TO SIDESTEP THESE BARRIERS.

Life in the Viceroyalty of Peru

The early years of the colonial period were turbulent and full of big changes, mostly for Tahuantinsuyo's former residents but also for the Spaniards. So when the conquistadores' disputes had been settled and the last Inca at Vilcabamba had been defeated (1571), the Viceroy Francisco de Toledo enacted regulations to ensure the Crown's total dominion over the Viceroyalty of Peru.

With these measures, daily life in the colony began taking shape and a new order was established. The native population were forced to leave their homes and move to cities called "reductions," and two distinct groups were created: the republic of Spaniards, which had greater privileges, and the republic of Indians, which served the Spanish.

Even though Toledo tried to separate the Spanish from the Indigenous people, they never stopped having contact. And so a society of great cultural complexity emerged, one in which different traditions—including those of the various African ethnic groups who had been taken into slavery—came together. This cultural richness could be seen in art and in popular celebrations like religious feasts and processions.

One of the most important festivals during the colonial period was the celebration of Corpus Christi in the city of Cuzco, the ancient capital of the Incan Empire. Spanish nobility participated alongside Incan nobility, who wore the elegant dress of "colonial Incas." The chiefs of groups like the Cañaris and Chachapoyas were seen as allies of the conquistadores and defenders of the Catholic faith, and so they marched dressed as "warrior angels" while the majority of the native people participated as spectators, porters, or musicians.

The feast was a reflection of life in the viceroyalty, where the luxuries and riches of one group of people coexisted alongside the servitude of the Indigenous majority and the slavery of native Africans.

EVERYTHING COMES TO AN END
The Incan standard-bearers' fabulous outfits—along with all reference to Tahuantinsuyo's grandeur—were banned following the rebellion of Túpac Amaru II in 1781. Spanish authorities wanted nothing more to do with the ancient rulers and became suspicious of their descendants, resulting in the loss of most of the Indigenous nobility's privileges.

INDIGENOUS NOBILITY
During the colonial period, descendants of the Incan rulers enjoyed certain privileges, which they earned by adapting to Spanish traditions. If they proved their nobility and they were baptized, they were spared from paying taxes and performing forced labor. It made sense to be Christian!

THE ROYAL INCAN STANDARD-BEARER
Families of the Incan nobility chose a representative or standard-bearer, who had the privilege of wearing a colonial version of the *mascaypacha*, which had once been a symbol of Tahuantinsuyo's supreme authority: the Sapa Inca.

THE CAÑARI STANDARD-BEARER
Groups like the Cañaris and Chachapoyas had a privileged position within the republic of Indians because they had been allies of the conquistadores since the very beginning. They served the Crown and had permission to use firearms. During the feast of Corpus Christi, the Cañari standard-bearer was the military equivalent of the royal Incan standard-bearer.

PAINTINGS OF CORPUS CHRISTI

THE CATHOLIC CHURCH ARRIVED IN THE AMERICAS WITH A MISSION TO CONVERT THE INDIGENOUS PEOPLE TO CHRISTIANITY. THAT'S WHY THEY BACKED THE CREATION OF RELIGIOUS IMAGES—VIRGINS, CRUCIFIXES, SAINTS, PROCESSIONS—AS A WAY OF SPREADING THEIR FAITH, INCLUDING A SERIES OF PAINTINGS OF THE FEAST OF CORPUS CHRISTI IN CUZCO. RESEARCHERS BELIEVE THESE PAINTINGS WERE CREATED BY NATIVE ARTISTS WHO PORTRAYED VARIOUS ANDEAN AUTHORITIES PROUDLY SPORTING INCAN INSIGNIA. THE CHURCH PERMITTED THESE IMAGES AS A WAY OF GETTING INDIGENOUS PEOPLE TO IDENTIFY MORE EASILY WITH THE CATHOLIC RELIGION. THE INCAN NOBILITY, IN TURN, USED THEM TO REAFFIRM THEIR STATUS WITHIN THE NEW COLONIAL ORDER.

DETAIL OF A PAINTING OF CORPUS CHRISTI, WHICH CAN BE FOUND IN THE MUSEUM OF RELIGIOUS ART IN CUZCO.

PAINTER: ANONYMOUS
MEDIUM: OIL ON CANVAS

* Illustration based on *Matrimonios de Martín de Loyola con Beatriz Ñusta y de Juan de Borja con Lorenza Ñusta de Loyola (Marriages of Martín de Loyola to Beatriz Ñusta and Juan de Borja to Lorenza Ñusta de Loyola)*. 1718. Anonymous. Pedro de Osma Museum.

COFRADÍAS
These special brotherhoods were devoted to particular saints and were in charge of carrying their floats during processions. It wasn't easy bearing statues of the Virgin and saints on your shoulders during the feast of Corpus Christi, but it was considered an honor!
CLERGY
During the colonial period, being religious was seen as a good thing. That's why many Spanish commoners chose to become monks or priests as a way of improving their status.
SPANISH NOBILITY
The nobility was made up of Spaniards and Creoles (those of Spanish descent). They were generally landowners, rich merchants, or the owners of mines or textile plants. They usually had noble titles like "marquess" and "earl."
AFRICANS AND THEIR DESCENDENTS
Africans arrived with the Europeans and were part of the republic of Spaniards. Over time, even within the colonial period, some managed to buy their freedom. Their workforce was incredibly important to the viceregal economy.
A MARRIAGE OF TWO NOBILITIES
Some members of the Spanish nobility joined the Incan nobility in marriage. The most famous of these bonds was that of Beatriz Ñusta—niece of Túpac Amaru I—and the Spanish captain Martín de Loyola—nephew of Saint Ignatius of Loyola. The Jesuit Order commissioned a painting of the ceremony on a large canvas in the Church of the Society of Jesus (in Cuzco) in 1741.

Remembering the Incas Today

Throughout the years, the Incas have sparked the imagination of everyone who learns about their history and traditions. They appear in books, movies, songs, artwork, fashion, and even in the name of a very famous Peruvian soda. Their memory lies in archaeological monuments that have resisted the passage of centuries and in artifacts held in museums; but it's also found in traditions that have been reinvented and kept alive, like the Inti Raymi—the most important celebration in the city of Cuzco.

Every June 24 since 1944, the people of Cuzco have taken part in the production of a great performance involving tens of thousands of people. The festivities of Inti Raymi—which means "Feast of the Sun" in Quechua—begin in Coricancha or the Temple of the Sun. They continue from there to the Plaza de Armas and end at the fortress of Sacsayhuamán, the main site of the event. The festival lasts seven hours, during which some 800 actors from Cuzco take on the roles of ancient residents of Tahuantinsuyo and their supreme rulers: the Sapa Inca and the *coya*.

Eight people carry the Inca aloft on a litter, and he is accompanied by a formidable entourage of warriors, dancers, maidens, and priests as he travels from place to place making ritual offerings. Coca leaves, alpacas, and llamas, among other things, are offered to the sun god in exchange for good harvests and the population's well-being. Although we don't know exactly what Inti Raymi was like at the time of Tahuantinsuyo, this new version is inspired by the texts of Garcilaso de la Vega and by a desire to rescue an ancestral tradition that, like the Incas, has become a symbol of Peruvian identity.

COUNTRY OF THE INCAS
When the viceroyalty ended, the Incas came to be seen as kings from an ancient, independent Peru, which had lost its freedom during the Spanish invasion and regained its autonomy in the new Republic. This vision of the Incas is part of why they later became a symbol of Peruvian identity.

THE INCAS IN WORLD CUISINE

PERU IS KNOWN FOR HAVING ONE OF THE MOST VARIED AND SOPHISTICATED CUISINES IN THE WORLD. ITS CONTRIBUTIONS INCLUDE 2,500 VARIETIES OF POTATO; 50 VARIETIES OF CORN; GRAINS LIKE QUINOA, AMARANTH, AND CAÑIHUA; AND MORE THAN 2,000 KINDS OF SWEET POTATO. ALL OF THESE FOODS ONCE FORMED AN IMPORTANT PART OF THE IMPERIAL PEOPLE'S DIET.

POTATO

Neo-Inka Museum by Susana Torres

* Illustration based on *Neo-Inka Museum*. 1999-2011. Collection of the Museo de Arte de Lima.

Knot by Jorge Eduardo Eielson

* Illustration based on *Knot*. 1973. Jorge Eielson. Collection of the Museo de Arte de Lima.

INCAS IN CONTEMPORARY ART AND DESIGN

THE INCAN EMPIRE AND PRE-COLOMBIAN DESIGNS HAVE ALSO INSPIRED VARIOUS WORKS OF CONTEMPORARY ART. THE POET AND VISUAL ARTIST JORGE EDUARDO EIELSON (1924–2006) DESIGNED HIS FAMOUS "NUDOS" (KNOTS) IN REFERENCE TO THE ANCIENT *QUIPUS*. ELENA IZCUE (1889–1970) REVIVED PRE-HISPANIC IMAGES AND SYMBOLS, APPLYING THEM TO DECORATIVE ART. AND SUSANA TORRES (LIMA, 1969) LOOKS AT INCAN CULTURE THROUGH POP ART IN HER MUSEUM PIECE MUSEO NEO-INKA (NEO-INKA MUSEUM).

ANDEAN STYLE

HEIRS TO THE INCAN TEXTILE TRADITION ARE NUMEROUS, BOTH AT A NATIONAL AND INTERNATIONAL LEVEL. AMONG THE MOST NOTABLE ARE THE RENOWNED WEAVER NILDA CALLAÑAUPA, FOUNDER OF THE CENTER FOR TRADITIONAL TEXTILES IN CUZCO, WHOSE MISSION IS TO PRESERVE THE HAND-WEAVING TRADITION AND ESTABLISH ASSOCIATIONS OF WEAVERS IN LOCAL COMMUNITIES. SAÚL ABEL CCARITA HAS REVIVED, AMONG OTHER THINGS, THE TRADITION OF WEAVING *TOCAPUS*. DESIGNERS LIKE MERCEDES CORREA AND CHIARA MACHIAVELLO, OF THE BRAND ESCVDO, HAVE TAKEN INSPIRATION FROM THE LEGACY OF ANCIENT INCAN TEXTILES FOR THEIR SPECTACULAR DESIGNS. TITI GIULFO WAS ONE OF THE FIRST DESIGNERS TO REVIVE THE BACKSTRAP LOOM. AT AN INTERNATIONAL LEVEL, THE CELEBRATED JOHN GALLIANO PRESENTED HIS COLLECTION, INSPIRED BY THE INCAN AND COLONIAL CLOTHING OF CUZCO, FOR THE FASHION HOUSE DIOR IN 2005.

SKIRTS OF ALL KINDS

The beautiful Andean skirts seen today in both regional dress and collections of casual clothing have evolved from the kirtle typically worn in sixteenth-century European courts. During the colonial period, this garment was produced using different fabrics, colors, ribbons, fretwork, and borders with Andean designs that enhanced their use and led to the regional variants we still see today.

ELEGANT FIBERS

Alpaca, vicuna, and native cotton—the principal materials of ancient Peru's woven fabrics—have reached international catwalks thanks to great designers like Karl Lagerfeld, Marc Jacobs, Stefano Tisci, and Carolina Herrera. Their value, their quality, and their history are recognized and appreciated throughout the entire world.

100%
BABY ALPACA

MADE IN PERU
FABRIQUÉ AU PÉROU

SINGING IN QUECHUA

YOUNG PERUVIAN ARTISTS LIKE RENATA FLORES (HUAMANGA, 2001) AND LIBERATO KANI (LIMA, 1993) SING THEIR SONGS IN QUECHUA, FOLLOWING IN THE FOOTSTEPS OF YMA SÚMAC (CAJAMARCA, 1922–CALIFORNIA, 2008), THE PERUVIAN SOPRANO WHO BROUGHT QUECHUA TO HOLLYWOOD. RENATA'S MUSIC MIXES TRAP AND POP WITH ANDEAN SOUNDS, WHILE LIBERATO KANI RAPS AND PERFORMS HIP HOP.

Glossary

Here we've gathered some Quechua words and their meanings to help you better understand the Incan world. They appear in the Hispanicized version (used throughout the text), with the original in parentheses.

Aclla/acllaconas (aklla/akllakuna)—Woman/women chosen from youth to serve the Inca. Their lives were dedicated to producing the finest textiles and making *chicha*, the ritual drink of Tahuantinsuyo.

Acllahuasi (akllawasi)—Compound where the *acllas* lived.

Aillu (ayllu)—Group of families thought to be descendants of a common ancestor who lived within a defined territory.

Anacu—A wrap dress fastened at the shoulder.

Apu (apu)—Ancestral spirit in the shape of a mountain, like Pumahuanca, Wañuymarca, Chumbivilcas and Ausangate.

Aquillas—Gold and silver cups made in pairs out of a single sheet of metal.

Callanca (kallanka)—Large rectangular structure with multiple entrances.

Camcha—Toasted corn.

Cancha (kancha)—Enclosed compound, usually made up of buildings surrounding a courtyard or plaza.

Chaquitaclla (chakitaqlla)—Farming tool invented in the Andes, which was used to plow land. It is also known as a foot plow.

Charqui—Salted and dried llama meat. *Charqui* is the origin of the English word jerky!

Chasqui (chaski)—A messenger during the Incan Empire who was in charge of carrying orders and announcements.

Chasquihuasi—A small house where a *chasqui* waited to run the next segment of the Inca Road.

Chicha—A drink made of fermented maize, which was sacred to the Incas. It is still a popular beverage in Latin America.

Chipana (chipana)—Bracelet.

Chumpi—A sash worn around the waists of Incan women.

Chuño—Dehydrated potatoes prepared by repeated freezing and thawing.

Chuspa (chuspa)—Small woven pouch that the Incas used to hold coca leaves and small amulets.

Cochas—Sunken fields used to increase farmland's humidity.

Colcas—Storehouses.

Conopa (qonopa)—Miniature plants and animals, usually made of stone, which were objects of worship and assured the fertility and abundance of the species they represented.

Coya—The principal wife of the Sapa Inca.

Cumbi (cumbi/cumpi)—High-quality decorated fabrics made by the Incas for the exclusive use of the elite.

Cumbicamayoc (cumbikamayoq)—Incan master weavers who, along with the *acllas*, specialized in the production of *cumbis.*

Hanan (hanan)—In Quechua, this refers to anything tall, high up, or elevated.

Huaca (wak'a)—Sacred creature, place, or thing (for example, shrines, idols, temples, tombs, mummies, animals, specific places, etc.).

Llacolla (llacolla)—Article of men's clothing, similar to a cape.

Llacta—City.

Lliclla (lliklla)—Article of women's clothing that covers the shoulders like a blanket.

Mallqui (mallki)—Quechua term for "plant," which also refers to the ancestor or founding father of an *aillu* and its territory. This is why Guamán Poma calls the mummies of the ancient Incan rulers *mallquis*.

Mamacona (mamakuna)—Older woman in charge of teaching and taking care of the young *acllas*. She too lived in the *acllahuasi*.

Mascaypacha (maskaypacha)—A headdress woven with golden thread and mountain caracara feathers, which was placed atop the Incan ruler's head to symbolize his great power.

Muyu (muyu)—Circle or circumference.

Paccha (paccha)—Watering device used by the Incas in religious ceremonies.

Panaca (panaca)—Noble families descended from the Incan rulers of the past.

Piki—Flea.

Pututu (pututu)—A conch-shell trumpet used by the *chasquis* and the Incan army.

Quero (kero)—Ceremonial cups, made in pairs, which were carved from a single block of wood.

Quipus—A system of cords and knots used by the Incas to record numerical data about goods, people, and workers. They were also used to record stories and historical facts.

Quipucamayoc (khipukamayoq)—An Incan government official in charge of the production and interpretation of *quipus*.

Qori or quri—Gold.

Suyo—Region.

Tambos (tampus)—Inns along the Inca Road where travelers could rest and resupply.

Tocapu—Geometric designs inside of little squares that decorated clothing and *quero*. Researchers believe that each *tocapu* had its own meaning.

Tucuyricuy—Supervisor of an Incan province; literally "he who observes."

Tupu (tupu)—Pin or broach.

Uncu (unku)—Article of men's clothing, similar to a tunic or shirt, which was worn by residents of the Incan empire.

Urin (urin)—Low (as opposed to *hanan*, which is high).

Urpu (urpu)—Incan jug.

Ushnu (ushnu)—Rectangular pyramid located on a flat terrace, on top of which different rituals were performed.

Waru waru—Raised fields used to protect crops from floods.

Bibliography

1. Adorno, R. (2002). *Un testigo de sí mismo. La integridad del manuscrito autógrafo* de El primer Nueva Corónica y buen gobierno de *Felipe Guamán Poma de Ayala* (1615/1616). http://www5.kb.dk/permalink/2006/poma/info/es/docs/index.htm
2. Alconini, S., & Covey, R. A. (eds.). (2018). *The Oxford handbook of the Incas*. Oxford University Press.
3. Amino, T. (2019). Los tres rostros del inca: concepciones y representaciones cambiantes de los incas durante el periodo colonial. In I. Shimada (ed.), *El imperio inka* (pp. 713-736). Lima: Fondo Editorial de la PUCP.
4. Artzi, B. A., Nir, A., & Santa Cruz, J. F. (2019). Los fragmentos de Vilcabamba, Perú: un testimonio iconográfico excepcional de la visión andina sobre el enfrentamiento entre indígenas y españoles. *Latin American Antiquity*, 30(1), 158-176.
5. Astete, F. H. (2017). *Los Incas y el poder de sus ancestros*. Fondo Editorial de la PUCP.
6. Astete, F. H., & Cerrón-Palomino, R. (eds.). (2016). *Juan de Betanzos y el Tahuantinsuyo: nueva edición de la* Suma y narración de los Incas. Lima: Fondo Editorial de la PUCP.
7. Baca, A. M., Pomalima, Y., & Téllez, S. (ed.). (2020). *El gran camino inca. Perú: integración y diversidad. Catálogo de la exposición itinerante (2020-2021)*. Lima: Ministerio de Cultura del Perú.
8. Banco Central de Reserva del Perú (BCRP). (n.d.). https://www.bcrp.gob.pe/docs/Transparencia/Notas-Informativas/2012/nota-informativa-2012-03-21.pdf
9. Bauer, B. S. (1999). The early ceramics of the Inca heartland. *Fieldiana*. Anthropology, 31, i-156. JSTOR, http://www.jstor.org/stable/29782643
10. Bauer, B. S., & Covey, R. A. (2002). Processes of state formation in the Inca heartland (Cuzco, Peru). *American Anthropologist*, 104(3), 846-864.
11. Bauer, B., & Smit, D. (2019). "Separando la paja del trigo". Mitos incas, leyendas incas y la evidencia arqueológica para el desarrollo del Estado en la región del Cuzco. In I. Shimada (ed.), *El imperio inka* (pp. 49-77). Lima: Fondo Editorial de la PUCP.
12. Betanzos, Juan de. (2010). *Suma y narración de los Incas, que los indios llamaron Capaccuna, que fueron Señores de la Ciudad del Cuzco y de todo lo a ella subjeto / escrita por Juan de Betanzos; publícala Marcos Jiménez de la Espada*. Alicante: Biblioteca Virtual Miguel de Cervantes; Madrid: Biblioteca Nacional. https://www.cervantesvirtual.com/nd/ark:/59851/bmccn7m9
13. Biblioteca Cervantes Virtual. (n.d.). http://cervantesvirtual.com. [Section dedicated to Inca Garcilaso de la Vega].
14. Cánepa Koch, G., Zuleta García, M., Hernández Macedo, M., & Biffi Isla, V. (2011). *Cocina e identidad: la culinaria peruana como patrimonio cultural inmaterial*. Lima: Ministerio de Cultura del Perú.
15. Canziani, J., Butters, L. J. C., Dam, P., Protzen, J. P., Wiersema, J., & Castillo, S. U. (2011). *Modelando el mundo: imágenes de la arquitectura precolombina*. Asociación Museo de Arte de Lima.
16. Castro, V., & Ceruti M. (2019). Los incas y el culto a las montañas de los Andes. In I. Shimada (ed.), *El imperio inka* (pp. 429-471). Lima: Fondo Editorial PUCP.
17. Cobo, B. (1892). *Historia del Nuevo Mundo* [1653] (ed. Marcos Jiménez de la Espada). Tomo III. Sevilla: Imp. de E. Rasco.
18. Covey, A. (2019). Intenciones del Imperio inca y realidades arqueológicas en la sierra de Perú. In I. Shimada (ed.), *El imperio inka* (pp. 151-171). Lima: Fondo Editorial de la PUCP.
19. Covey, R. A. (2021). The Inca Empire. En P. Fibiger Bang, C. A. Bayly & W. Scheidel (eds.), *The Oxford world history of empire*. Vol. 2: *The history of empires*. New York. (online ed.: Oxford Academic). https://doi.org/10.1093/oso/9780197532768.003.0025
20. Cummins, T. (2004). *Brindis con el Inca. La abstracción andina y las imágenes coloniales de los queros*. Lima: Fondo Editorial de la UNMSM.
21. Cummins, T. (2019). Arte incaico. In I. Shimada (ed.), *El imperio inka* (pp. 279-328). Lima: Fondo Editorial de la PUCP.
22. Curatola, M. (2009, 6 de mayo). Los oráculos del antiguo Perú [interview with Marco Curatola] .edu. https://puntoedu.pucp.edu.pe/voces-pucp/los-oraculos-delantiguo-peru/
23. Chacaltana, S., Arkush, E., & Marcone G. (eds.) (2017). *Nuevas tendencias en el estudio de los caminos*. Lima: Ministerio de Cultura – Proyecto Qhapaq Ñan.
24. Del Busto, J. A. (2004). *Conquista y Virreinato*. Enciclopedia Temática del Perú, tomo II. Lima: Empresa Editora El Comercio.
25. Del Busto, J. A. (2011a). *La Conquista del Perú*. Lima: Empresa Editora El Comercio.
26. Del Busto, J. A. (2011b). *Los hijos del Sol y Túpac Yupanqui, descubridor de Oceanía*. Lima: Empresa Editora El Comercio.
27. Det Kongelige Bibliotek–Guamán Poma Site. (n.d.). http://www5.kb.dk/permalink/2006/poma/info/es/frontpage.htm
28. Earls, J. (2006). *La agricultura andina ante una globalización en desplome*. Lima: Pontificia Universidad Católica del Perú. Centro de Investigaciones Sociológicas, Económicas, Políticas y Antropológicas (CISEPA).
29. Earls, J., & Cervantes, G. (2019). Cosmología inca en Moray. Astronomía, agricultura y peregrinaje. In I. Shimada (ed.), *El imperio inka* (pp. 211-254). Lima: Fondo Editorial de la PUCP.
30. Garcilaso de la Vega, I. (2010). *Comentarios reales de los incas*. Colección Biblioteca Imprescindibles Peruanos. Lima: Empresa Editora El Comercio.
31. Humboldt, A. (1896). *Sites des cordillères et monuments des peuples indigènes de l'Amérique*. París: Legrand, Pomey et Crouzet.
32. INEI [Instituto Nacional de Estadística e Informática]. (2018). *Censos Nacionales XII de Población y VII de Vivienda, 22 de octubre del 2017. Perú: resultados definitivos*. Lima.

33. Itier, C. (2019). ¿Qué significaba el término inka? *Bulletin de l'Institut Français d'Études Andines* [online], 48(2).http://journals.openedition.org/bifea/10587 https://doi.org/10.4000/bifea.10587
34. Julien, C. J. (2018). *Para leer la historia Inca*. Lima: Ediciones El Lector.
35. Kauffmann Doig, F. (2019). *Gentilmantarimay*: La función que desempeñaban los intihuatanas, como el de Machu Picchu. *Revista Yachay*, 8(1).
36. Kaulicke, P. (2019). Conceptos incaicos de vida, muerte y culto a los ancestros. In I. Shimada (ed.), *El imperio inka* (pp. 407-428). Lima: Fondo Editorial de la PUCP.
37. Kusunoki, R., Pardo, C., & Rucabado, J. (2023). *Los Incas. Más allá de un Imperio*. Lima: Museo de Arte de Lima.
38. Lumbreras, L. G. (2012). El adoratorio de Saywite o Concacha. *Revista Moneda*, (151), 48-50.
39. Ministerio de Cultura del Perú. (n.d.). *Qhapaq* Ñan [online]. http://caminantesqn.cultura.pe
40. Murra, J. (1975). *Formaciones económicas y políticas del mundo andino*. Lima: IEP.
41. Museo de Arte de Lima (MALI). (2022). *Genealogía de los incas*. [Video].
42. Nair, S., & Protzen J. (2019). Arquitectura y paisaje inca: variación, tecnología y simbolismo. In I. Shimada (ed.), *El imperio inka* (pp. 357-384). Lima: Fondo Editorial de la PUCP.
43. Niles, S. (2019). Considerando las fincas reales de los incas: arquitectura, economía, historia. In I. Shimada (ed.), *El imperio inka* (pp. 385-406). Lima: Fondo Editorial de PUCP.
44. Pavez, A. M., Recart, C., & Hojas, I. (2010). *Sabores de América*. Santiago: Editorial Amanuta.
45. Pease, F. (1991). Los incas. Lima: Fondo Editorial PUCP.
46. Phipps, E. (2019). Tradiciones textiles de los incas y sus contrapartes coloniales. In I. Shimada (ed.), *El imperio inka* (pp. 49-77). Lima: Fondo Editorial de la PUCP.
47. Pizarro, P. (1986 [1571]). *Relación del descubrimiento y conquista de los reinos del Perú.* Lima: Pontificia Universidad Católica del Perú.
48. Planas, E. (2013). *Perú: moda y textiles. Peru: Fashion and Textiles*. Lima: Comisión de Promoción del Perú para la Exportación y el Turismo (PromPerú).
49. Rodríguez Garrido, J. (2010). *Felipe Guamán Poma de Ayala: El primer* Nueva corónica y buen gobierno. [Selection and spelling updates by José A. Rodríguez Garrido, using the transcription and edition of John V. Murra, Rolena Adorno y Jorge L. Urioste, corrected by Ivan Boserup y R. Adorno]. Biblioteca Imprescindibles Peruanos. Lima: Empresa Editora El Comercio.
50. Rostworowski, M. (1992). *Historia del Tahuantinsuyo.* Lima: Instituto de Estudios Peruanos (IEP).
51. Salomon, F. (2019). Los incas a través de los textos: las fuentes primarias. In I. Shimada (ed.), *El imperio inka* (pp. 49-77). Lima: Fondo Editorial de la PUCP.
52. Tord, M. (ed.). (2020). *Rutas ancestrales del Qhapaq* Ñan. Lima: Ministerio de Cultura.
53. Urton, G. (2019). El estado de las cuerdas: administración de los quipus en el Imperio incaico. In I. Shimada (ed.), *El imperio inka* (pp. 255-278). Lima: Fondo Editorial de la PUCP.
54. Van Kessel, J., Earls, J., Grillo, E., & Araujo, H. (1990). *Tecnología andina: una introducción*. La Paz: HISBOL.
55. Vetter, L. M. (2008). *Plateros indígenas en el Virreinato del Perú: siglos XVI y XVII.* Lima: Fondo Editorial de la UNMSM y Minas Buenaventura S. A. A.
56. Vetter, L. M. (2014). El uso del metal en las culturas precolombinas. *Moneda,* 157 48-52.
57. Williams, P. (2017). Una perspectiva comparada de los caminos wari y tiwanaku: los antecedentes del Qhapaq Ñan incaico. In S. Chacaltana, G. Marcone & E. Arkush (eds.), *Nuevas tendencias en el estudio de los caminos. Conferencia Internacional en el Ministerio de Cultura. 26–27 June 2014* (pp. 30-47). Lima, Perú: Proyecto Qhapaq Ñan – Sede Nacional, Ministerio de Cultura.
58. World Heritage Convention – UNESCO. (n.d.) http://whc.unesco.org. [Page about Lake Titicaca].
59. Wuffarden, L. (2005). La descendencia real y el "renacimiento inca" en el virreinato. In *Los incas, reyes del Perú* (pp. 174-251). Lima: BCP.
60. Wuffarden, L. (2020). La memoria de los incas en el Corpus Christi del Cuzco. In *Arte imperial Inca: sus orígenes y transformaciones desde la Conquista a la Independencia* (pp. 132-163). Lima: BCP.

GUAMÁN POMA DE AYALA:

1. Royal Danish Library, GKS 2232 kvart: Guamán Poma, *Nueva corónica y buen gobierno* (c. 1615), page [120].
2. Royal Danish Library, GKS 2232 kvart: Guamán Poma, *Nueva corónica y buen gobierno* (c. 1615), page [366].
3. Royal Danish Library, GKS 2232 kvart: Guamán Poma, *Nueva corónica y buen gobierno* (c. 1615), page [256].
4. Royal Danish Library, GKS 2232 kvart: Guamán Poma, *Nueva corónica y buen gobierno* (c. 1615), page [1147].
5. Royal Danish Library, GKS 2232 kvart: Guamán Poma, *Nueva corónica y buen gobierno* (c. 1615), page [263].
6. Royal Danish Library, GKS 2232 kvart: Guamán Poma, *Nueva corónica y buen gobierno* (c. 1615), page [390].
7. Royal Danish Library, GKS 2232 kvart: Guamán Poma, *Nueva corónica y buen gobierno* (c. 1615), page [86].
8. Royal Danish Library, GKS 2232 kvart: Guamán Poma, *Nueva corónica y buen gobierno* (c. 1615), page [132].
9. Royal Danish Library, GKS 2232 kvart: Guamán Poma, *Nueva corónica y buen gobierno* (c. 1615), page [130].
10. Royal Danish Library, GKS 2232 kvart: Guamán Poma, *Nueva corónica y buen gobierno* (c. 1615), page [1132].
11. Royal Danish Library, GKS 2232 kvart: Guamán Poma, *Nueva corónica y buen gobierno* (c. 1615), page [975].

1.

2.

3.

4.

5.

6.

7.

8.

9.

10.

11.